SCREEN PRINTING : DESIGN & TEC

SCREEN PRINTING:
Design & Technique

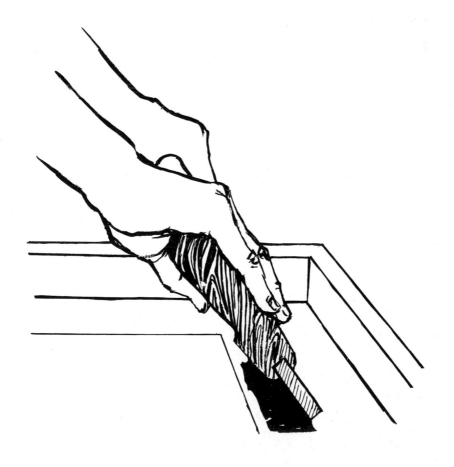

SCREEN PRINTING:
Design & Technique

NICHOLAS BRISTOW

B.T. Batsford Ltd, London

ISBN 0 7134 5812 7

Printed in Hong Kong
for the publishers
B.T. Batsford Ltd
4 Fitzhardinge Street
London W1H 0AH

Acknowledgements
My thanks to Simon Marshall for all his help and to Chris
Betambeau of Advanced Graphics.

The majority of the photographs by Andrew Marshall.

CONTENTS

INTRODUCTION

Design for screen printing

The main advantage of screen printing is that it can be operated on a number of different levels. Starting with items of material found in any household and a few simple home-made bits and pieces, one can print on the kitchen table; Chris Prater, who founded Kelpra, which became a landmark in fine art screen printing, did just that in 1957.

Even with this most basic equipment it is possible to produce good, exciting and even quite sophisticated designs with practice. Whether you keep your experiments to working on paper, or develop to printing on material, there is little difference to the procedure.

For a small sum, it is possible to modify this simple system to cope with finer detail and editioning, etc. and even use the expertise and sophistication of the advanced technology on offer these days.

The origin of screen printing from stencils

Throughout history people have sought ways of duplicating images. Stencil printing is one of the earliest known methods. From ancient times patterns have been pierced out of such materials as leaves; colours or dyes were then dabbed through the perforations to achieve a simple printed design.

As times progressed, various cultures, especially the Japanese, greatly refined the process. One major difficulty was that isolated parts of the design had to be supported. This meant that supporting bridges had to be cut into the stencil which, as the sophistication of designs increased, resulted in unwanted and clumsy effects. To overcome this problem, the Japanese devised a way of holding the various parts of a stencil in place by means of a network of human hair. This was later replaced by threads of silk.

The use of silk threads to attach intricate parts of stencils may have led to the eventual use of silk cloth as a complete stencil support. This took place in the latter half of the nineteenth century. Towards the end of the century, Japanese art and design became highly fashionable in Europe, and this helped to establish screen printing as an art form. During the early years of this century, screen printed textiles became more widespread. By 1915 the first photographic silk screen process was developed, which rapidly led to a wider commercial use into such areas as graphic art.

Screen printing process

Screen printing is a stencil method of printing. The difference between ordinary stencil printing and screen printing is that in screen printing the stencil is held in place and supported, which allows small areas which are isolated from the stencil, and detail, to be printed. To achieve this, the stencil is attached to the back of a screen of tightly-stretched material. The material, originally silk, consists of a fine threadwork of open weave. Ink is forced through the weave of the material and open areas of the stencil onto the surface to be printed by means of a tool with a flexible blade, called a squeegee (*Fig. 1*)

The image that is printed, as with any stencil, is the exact opposite of the stencil used. The stencil itself forms a barrier through which ink cannot penetrate. In other words, a stencil takes on much the same role as a negative does in black and white photography. The tones are reversed in the processing, in this case printing. For instance, if you wish to print a square shape, you carefully cut a square out of a sheet of newspaper and use what's left of the sheet of newspaper as the stencil. In other words, you start off with a *negative design*. This may sound complicated, but in practice one soon becomes accustomed to it, until it becomes second nature.

There are, however, methods which enable you to start off working with a *positive design*. Due to various substances resisting others and chemical changes, it is possible to form positive images that can be naturally reversed in stencil form, so that they print to the same tonal exactness of the original. These methods are fully explained in later chapters.

If a single word were to be used to sum up the qualities of screen printing, it would probably be 'flexibility'. The process can be used to print on either small or vast-sized formats. It can be used to print on a wide range of different surfaces and materials including paper, card, fabrics, plastics, metal, wood, glass and ceramics. It is also possible to print on various thicknesses of material. These qualities have allowed screen printing to become a popular form of printing in many industries. Commercially, screen printing is widely used on fabrics, ceramics, plastics, packaging and in advertising. In the relatively short time of diversifying from a humble beginning, numerous adaptations and advancements have come about. Whilst these have been directed towards the commercial uses of the process, many of them are just as useful to the amateur fine art printer and commercial user alike.

1   *Making a print*

1 A SIMPLE START

From an equipment point of view, screen printing is the 'do-it-yourself' form of print-making. Whereas most other forms of printing rely on heavy, specialized and often expensive equipment such as presses, everything required for starting in screen printing can be packed into a couple of lightweight cardboard boxes. The few simple items needed to begin with can easily be home-made, or adapted from commonplace odds and ends. For those of you with little time, or inclination, to adapt equipment, a complete range of products is readily available, both as single items, or as packaged systems.

In addition to these favourable economic and practical considerations, the medium is also very flexible, and it is possible to devise a system to work in almost any space available. Whereas the smallest area can be used for producing card-sized prints, large screens can just as readily be made up for coping with oversize images.

SIMPLE EQUIPMENT

One most important requirement is the need for a good secure working and printing surface of a workable height. The surface of this needs to be perfectly flat. A sturdy kitchen table, covered with newspaper, makes an ideal

2   *Equipment for printing*

The following is a list of the equipment you will need to start screen printing		
Wooden frame	Scissors	Cotton rags
Organdie	Scalpel	Newsprint paper
Squeegee	Drawing pins	Varnish
Screwtop jars	(or staple gun)	String
Spoons	Cellulose paste	Pegs or paper clips
Palette knife	Poster paints	Cartridge paper
Sponge	Spoons	Paper parcel tape

surface. Most laminated kitchen working tops can just as easily be used. In both cases, you will find that having a water supply and sink close to hand can be very useful.

The frame

The purpose of the frame is to act as a support, over which the organdie (mesh) is stretched. To be serviceable, the frame needs to be sturdy and of a rigid construction. Any flexing would result in poor-quality printing and hopeless registration of colours. A good test of a frame is that it should rest evenly on a flat surface. If one or two of the corners appear raised in this position, it is doubtful whether the screen will print evenly.

As well as holding the stencil in place, the screen acts as a reservoir for the ink during printing. Ample space on either side of the stencil is needed during printing in order to retain the ink.

Making the frame

For the purpose of explaining the printing process, I have taken a particular frame size as my example throughout this description. A frame of 60 × 60cm (24 × 24in) would provide a useful average-size proportion to start with. For this, use planed timber of 5 × 2.5cm (2 × 1in) dimensions, obtainable from any woodyard. The 5cm (2in) measurement represents the height of the frame section, ensuring rigidity. When selecting the wood, look for knot-free lengths and reject any appearing warped through poor storage. After cutting the four sides, join the corners adequately to prevent movement. Fig. 3 shows some simple methods of joining the corners.

(a) The easiest way of joining the corners is with straight cuts, glued and nailed together and further reinforced with angle irons screwed to the top. Make sure the butted end of the joint has been cut square, otherwise the frame may go out of alignment.

(b) A simple, yet more robust joint allows the wood to be glued and nailed on two edges.

(c) A strong and easy alternative for joining corners is to use mitre cuts, similar to those used in picture framing. These can be reinforced with

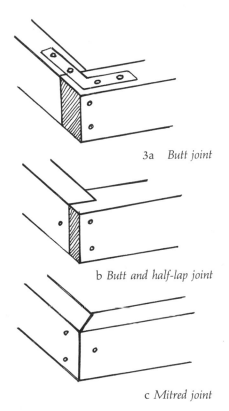

3a *Butt joint*

b Butt and half-lap joint

c Mitred joint

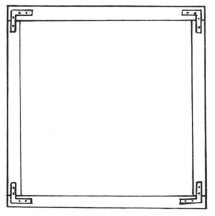

Angle irons can be used to give any wooden frame rigidity

angle irons after gluing and nailing. Nail and glue the frame together on a flat surface. This will ensure that it does not end up askew and out of alignment. The finished frame will need to be sandpapered for easy

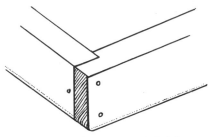

4 *Sandpaper the frame and slightly bevel the bottom outside edge, so that the organdie will not be snagged*

handling, and the outside bottom edges (*Fig. 4*) slightly bevelled so as not to snag the organdie as it is stretched over the frame.

Finally, apply a liberal coat of varnish to the finished frame. This will prevent the wood from getting wet when washing out the screen, and ensure against future warping.

Using a wooden picture frame
There is usually at least one picture framer in any large town. For a small amount he should be able to cut and make up a frame for you, though you will possibly have to supply the 5cm (2in) wood.

Another alternative is to use a secondhand wooden picture frame. Suitable sturdy examples can often be obtained from junk shops.

The screen fabric

The screen fabric needs to be of a fine, open weave to allow ink to be squeezed through the mesh to the underlying print surface. The overall strength of the fabric must be such that it stands up to being stretched tautly over the frame and does not sag when wet.

Silk was originally used for this purpose, but these days silk has largely been replaced by a number of synthetic fabrics which offer greater resilience and improved properties. For our purposes cotton organdie provides a cheap, serviceable material with which to make a start. Make sure you buy *cotton* organdie and not *nylon*, which stretches and sags when wet. If it is difficult to obtain locally, see the list of suppliers on p. 158 for suggestions.

Stretching the screen fabric
Unroll the organdie on a table top and place the frame upon it. The weave of the material should run parallel to the sides of the frame. Cut a square of material, allowing approximately 7.5cm (3in) on all sides. The material can now be fastened to the frame by using drawing pins or a staple gun. It is important that the organdie should be stretched evenly over the frame. To ensure you get an even tension follow the procedure below, and refer to Fig. 5.

Place the frame over the organdie, adjusting to ensure that there is about the same amount of overlapping organdie on each side. Turn up one edge of organdie and drawing pin it to the centre of one side of the frame. Place two further pins on

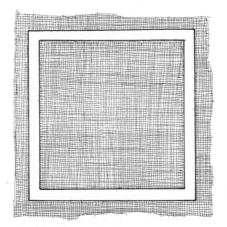
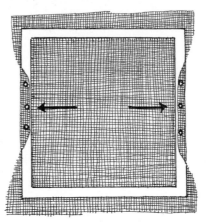
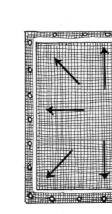

5   *Stretching the screen fabric*

either side of the first one, about 7.5cm (3in) apart. As you do this, pull gently towards the corners for tension.

Now fasten the centre of the opposite side, pulling the organdie tightly across the frame as you do so. It is important to pull the material really tight, but to do so steadily so as not to tear it. Fasten the other two pins as before, then secure the centres of the other two sides in a similar fashion.

With about the same 7.5cm (3in) between pins, secure the

remaining material by working towards the corners. As you do so, pull firmly towards the corner you are working to. This should create an even tension across the screen.

Although the organdie is now fully stretched, you may possibly have to improve the tension at this stage. By working from the centre outwards, on opposite sides, pull the organdie tighter between the pins, securing with new pins, or staples, as you do so.

The finished result should be

tight and even, like a drum skin. Any slackness would result in the stencil moving during printing, spoiling the printed result. If the surface is not tight on completion, it may be possible, by removing some of the pins, to retighten and secure the areas affected. Failing this, remove the pins and start afresh. Never make do with a poorly-stretched screen.

Masking the edges and making a waterproof border

Once the screen is stretched, the inside edges will need to be masked. This is done to prevent ink seeping underneath during printing and marking the results. At the same time, a waterproof border around the edges is needed to act as an ink reservoir later on. Brown gummed paper tape, bought in 5cm (2in) wide rolls, is ideal for both purposes.

Cut four 56cm (22in) strips (the internal size of the frame). Fold these in half along the length and wet them under a tap. Then secure them to the inside edges of the frame, half on the wood and half against the organdie (*Fig. 6*). Carefully dab a sponge along the inner edges to remove air bubbles and wrinkles.

Turn the frame over and apply overlapping strips of tape on the back to form a masked border of 10cm (4in) width all round (*Fig. 7*). Smooth these flat with a damp sponge.

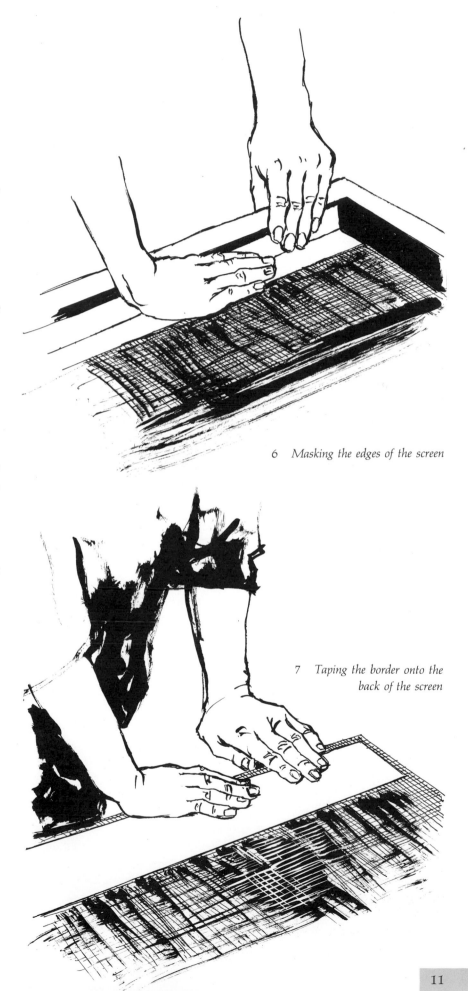

6 *Masking the edges of the screen*

7 *Taping the border onto the back of the screen*

When dry, waterproof both sides of the taped-off margins and taped inside edges by applying two coats of varnish.

Squeegee (printing blade)

The only specialized piece of equipment you may need to buy to start with is the blade (squeegee). A squeegee consists of a strip of rubber, or polythene, usually 5cm (2in) wide and 1cm ($\frac{3}{8}$in) thick, set in a wood, or metal, holder. It can be purchased complete from screen printing suppliers and is usually priced by the inch. A cheaper solution is to buy a length of rubber strip from the supplier and make your own wooden holder. The easiest way of doing this is by using three separate lengths of wood (*Fig. 8*).

As a third, even cheaper, alternative, items such as rubber

window cleaning wipers, or plastic draught-excluder strips, can be used effectively for simple printing. These can also prove useful when printing an isolated part of a design in a particular colour and a smaller blade is needed.

The size of the blade has to be shorter than the inside measurement of the frame, with added space allowed for manoeuvring.

For the size frame I have suggested to start with (60 × 60cm [24 × 24in]), buy a 45cm (18in) squeegee.

Printing inks

Although there is a wide range of screen printing inks available these days, to start with you may find it easier and cheaper to make your own. Cellulose wallpaper paste makes an excellent cheap base into which you can mix poster colours, or other water-based paint and ink.

Using cellulose paste and poster paint

It is easier to premix ample paste and add colours to it later. For mixing, use a large jar, or a plastic bucket. Add the water first, then gradually stir in the paste granules. Leave to stand for an hour or more to ensure that the paste granules have totally absorbed the water. Thoroughly stir the mixture, which should be of the consistency of double cream. If you make it too runny it may

bleed under the edges of the stencil during printing and mark the paper.

When the paste is mixed, you can transfer it to smaller screw-top jars. Add the required colours gradually, stirring in well. Poster colours etc. may need to be thinned with water before being added to the paste.

Unused colours can be stored for a considerable time in screw-top jars with the lids on. In such cases, an occasional stirring helps to prevent mould from forming on the top.

Simple paper stencils

The easiest and quickest way of making a screen print is by using simple torn, or cut, paper stencils (*Figs 9 and 10*). Using this method will allow you more time to familiarize yourself with the printing procedures. You should be able to get into a rhythm of making simple prints without getting too weighed down with technicalities of design.

For these first experiments, it is likewise a good idea not to base your designs on a realistic, or semi-figurative, motif (*Fig. 11*). Rather, form your designs around the possibilities of the variety of shapes that can be torn, or cut, at random from sheets of newspaper. As this is a quick procedure, cut and tear many more shapes than you are likely to use, concentrating on producing a wide variety of

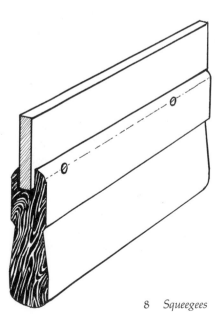

8   Squeegees

9a   Cut and tear out a few small single shapes and arrange them on the printing format. This will allow the first light printed areas, shown here as black, to print extensively

b As you overprint with further colours, allow for the stencil to cover a larger area. This will give the best effect of overprinting

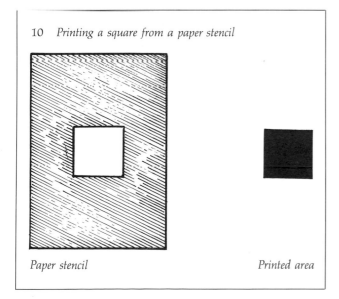

10   Printing a square from a paper stencil

Paper stencil   Printed area

sizes and shapes. After this, place a toned sheet of paper, like sugar paper or wrapping paper, a little larger in size than your frame, on a table and mark out a 40cm (16in) square in the centre. This drawn-out area represents the printing area of your screen.

Arrange some of the shapes you have cut, or torn, on the square. They can be freely

11   Landscape by Maria Mathers. The overprinted effect of using a few paper stencils can produce striking results

moved around until they form an interesting-looking pattern. The white of the newsprint will show up well against the toned background paper. Cut away any parts of shapes that overlap the square by more than 1.2cm ($\frac{1}{2}$in). You are now ready to print. The paper shapes on the square will stick to the back of the screen after the first pull of ink and form your first stencil.

HOW TO PRINT

Negative effects of stencils
Remember that the shapes you have cut and torn out and positioned will form the negative parts of the print: they are the parts of the design that will not print. It is the surrounding areas of the 40cm (16in) square, where the background paper is visible, that will take on the colour.

Printing the first colour
Carefully lower your screen onto the toned paper, so that the taped edges are in alignment with the marked-out square. Using the lightest colour you have mixed, perhaps a yellow, spoon out a ridge of this along the top border of your screen, keeping it away from the inside edge of the frame (*Fig. 12*). The ink should have been mixed thick enough for it not to run within the border. To prevent the frame from moving during printing, it is advisable to have a second person to hold down the top

12　*Spoon out a line of ink along the top border of your screen, making sure to keep it away from the inside edge of the border*

outside edges of the frame when printing. This is only necessary when a simple frame is used and does not apply when a baseboard is added, as detailed in Chapter 2.

With the ink now along the border furthest away from you, pick up the squeegee. Hold it with both hands at an angle of 45 degrees to the frame, with the leading edge of the blade resting on the organdie just behind the ink (*Fig. 13*).

Pull the blade towards you in a firm, constant movement, with the leading edge of the blade pressing down on the screen (*Fig. 14*). As the blade is pulled across the screen, a certain amount of the ink, preceding it, will be forced through the mesh of the organdie to form a print.

The ink from this first 'pull' will have stuck the paper cut-outs, forming the stencil, to the screen. Gently raise the screen

and push back the ink; recharge the screen with ink and reposition the ink for the second pull (*Fig. 15*).

Lift the frame off the first sugar paper print and replace this paper with a sheet of cartridge paper. Repeat the printing process until you have five or six prints.

After printing, use a palette knife, or spoon, to scrape ink from the squegee back into the jar. Likewise, most of the screen ink can be scooped up using the flat edge of a palette knife. Be careful not to snag the organdie when doing this. With most of the ink returned, peel the pieces of paper stencil from the back of the screen, and wash the screen out under a cold tap. Rub lightly over the back of the screen with a sponge, keeping the water running, to ensure all ink is cleared from the mesh. If there is one available, a garden hose or shower attachment is an efficient way of thoroughly cleaning a screen.

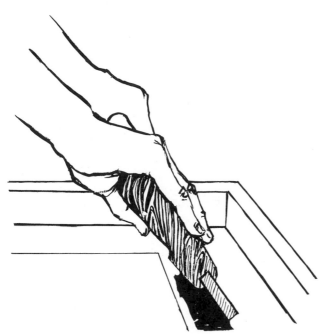

13 *Position the squeegee at an angle of 45 degrees.*

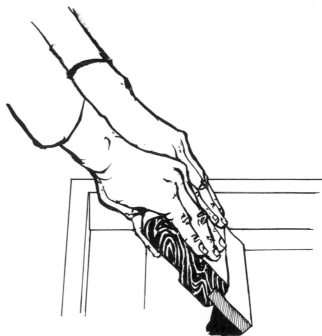

14 *In a constant motion, keeping even pressure, pull the squeegee across the screen towards you until you reach the near border*

Once the last traces of ink have been washed from the screen, it can be left to dry, ready for the next colour. A fan heater is useful in cutting down the drying time. Cellulose (wallpaper) paste inks dry quickly, making it possible to print several colours in a morning or afternoon.

Using the extra paper shapes you cut, rearrange them within the square of the first print. Try placing them in opposing positions to the first shapes, so that they half overlap. Continually overlapping the shapes could result in a more interesting overall print, incorporating a greater number of overprinted colours and incidental shapes.

Printing further colours

With the shapes for the second stencil arranged, repeat the printing procedure using the next lightest colour, perhaps an orange or brown (*Fig. 16*). After printing two or more colours, the effects of overprinting

15 *Reposition the ink for a second pull*

should look interesting and probably quite different from those expected. With darker colours, try using larger paper shapes as stencils, so that you only print through small sections of the screen. If this is not done, you may find much of what you have achieved earlier is obliterated by the darker colours.

Because the format of the print is square, you can obtain innumerable variations of pattern by turning the screen around and printing some of the colours upside down, etc.

THE EFFECT OF OVERPRINTING WITH TRANSPARENT COLOURS

The effect of using poster paint mixed with a cellulose binder should provide you with a range of reasonably-transparent colours. To make maximum gain of this, it is worth while adopting a working procedure not dissimilar to that used in watercolour painting. Put simply, instead of thinking in terms of isolated areas of colour placed next to each other, you plan your print, taking into consideration a build-up of several layers of overlaid transparent colour. This is not as difficult as it may sound. It requires starting with light colours, continuing with medium-toned ones and finishing with any bright or dark colours you may want. As with the watercolour technique, print large areas of light colours, smaller areas of half tone, and smaller areas still of dark colours.

If prints become too dark, it is possible, by adding white poster paint to light mixes, to lighten them by overprinting in

16   Daisies *by Maria Mathers. Simple overprinted results from using cut and torn paper stencils*

opaque colours. In small areas this can look very effective, though when overdone the results can appear dull and heavy.

BLENDED COLOURS

Although the natural results of screen printing are flat printed colour areas, it is possible to print several different colours at a time in the form of a blend. Using this method, you can produce areas of colour which fade from one to the other in an uninterrupted way.

To achieve this, position ridges of the different colours next to each other along the screen margin. Hold the squeegee as for printing, and with short gentle chopping motions mix the inks with the leading edge of the blade. Move the squeegee slightly from side to side when doing this to hasten the mixing process. You will see from the appearance of the line of ink when the colours have totally mixed. The gradation of colour will become visible. Before using good paper, however, try a print on newspaper to ensure the blend is thoroughly mixed. If it is somewhat streaky, you will find that a few more pulls using newspaper should rectify this.

A variation on blending different colours is to use a clear binder, in this case cellulose paste, placed next to one colour and mixed in the

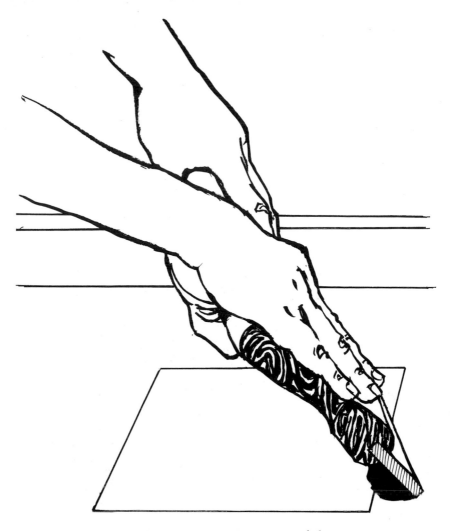

17   *Provided that ample screen space exists around the stencil format, the blend can be set at any angle to the print*

same way, thus achieving a faded-out effect. Colour that is dark on one part of the stencil can be phased out gradually to become transparent elsewhere.

As well as producing attractive effects, blending and fading out with clear binder can at times help to resolve problems with unwanted or clumsy parts of stencils. Any part of a stencil which, when printed, looks awkward can be softened, or faded out completely in this way.

As the line of the blend, or fade out, follows the movement of the blade, only straight line directions are possible. For instance, one cannot create curved blended results.

However, if the printing area is small in relation to the screen, to allow for manoeuvrability, the direction of the blend can be set at any angle to the print (*Fig. 17*). Added to this, the direction of further blends can be set at different angles, providing extra variety.

This technique is most suited to dealing with large printed areas that are plain, where a little variation of tone and colour could improve the design. Skies and expanses of water can readily be enhanced in this way. A sky can easily be changed from a cool blue at the top to a warm pearly grey towards the horizon.

For smooth blends it is important to mix colours to an even thickness. If one is more liquid, it will spread more quickly than a thicker one, creating difficulties. Even when you have mastered the technique, you will find subtle differences with each print taken. The colours of a blend gradually spread more into each other, until they become so intermixed that the blended effect is altogether lost. Before this happens, you will have to adjust the mix by adding more colour.

PICTURE PRINTS USING OIL PASTELS

This method of working, embodying the use of oil pastels, is far more akin to painting and drawing than any form of print-making. It requires the use of neither stencils, nor separate overprinted colours. Instead, an entire picture can be built up, using any number or combination of colours, by drawing directly onto the screen. A coarse screen fabric, such as organdie, is ideally suited for this process. The coarseness of the organdie allows the pastels to be grated against the weave, to deposit a thick layer of pigment in the open mesh.

Procedure for making a print
To start with, place the screen against a firm, flat support, such as a drawing board. For clarity, a sheet of white paper with, if necessary, an outline sketch of the image, can be positioned between the board and the

screen (*Fig. 18*). Then, by drawing directly onto the organdie, you can start to form an image. Different colours can be overlaid, or cross-hatched, in a similar fashion to that used in pastel painting technique. As the colours quickly dissipate during printing, it pays to build up a really strong image before considering printing. It also helps to lift the screen occasionally to see how much pastel has been deposited. There is usually less than you think. Try to avoid leaving too many areas of untreated screen. These areas may look attractive on the screen, but are likely to give an unfinished appearance to the final result.

The finished image can be printed in the normal fashion, either by using a clear-based oil binder, or certain emulsion binders. Helizarin binder, a water-soluble emulsion, has a thick, creamy consistency, making it ideal for this type of printing. The white spirit in the emulsion enables the oil pastel to become soft, without liquefying.

The first print taken will probably be the least successful. According to the amount of oil pastel in the screen mesh, it may print patchily or very heavily. After the first pull, recharge the screen and wait for about half a minute before printing the second copy. This will allow time for the binder on the screen to penetrate and

soften the oil pastels.

According to the strength of the image, it should be possible to make up to about ten impressions. After the usually harsh first pull, impressions take on soft blended characteristics, not dissimilar to that of pastel drawings. The overall soft texture, a result of the screen mesh being visible, can add further to the print quality. With each print taken, the image becomes fainter, until the oil pastel on the screen has finally been used up. As the thickness of pigment deposited on the screen will vary considerably, parts of the image will fade, or disappear, whilst areas of thicker deposit remain relatively strong. This variance, rather than detracting, can add to the subtlety and atmosphere of the image.

After, say, half a dozen impressions have been taken, the prints will become uniformly faint. At this stage, it is possible to add to the screen image with further pastel work. Try dipping the ends of the oil pastels into the binder before attempting to draw with them; this should soften them, making it easier to draw into the existing image. Also, recharge the screen with binder before starting to rework the drawing. A recharged screen should allow you a good few minutes before the binder starts to dry in. In this way you can keep an image printing almost

18   *Sketching onto the organdie with oil pastels*

indefinitely, strengthening each part of the image before it wears out. Apart from strengthening the existing design, you can experiment with different colours, gradually changing the entire colour scheme and altering the drawing as you proceed.

Certain natural changes will also take place. With each impression taken, closely-aligned colours will tend to blend into each other. A certain amount of colour will also mix with the binder, which in time will print as a light colour.

Using a transparent coloured binder

As an effective addition to this process, a transparent coloured binder can be used in place of a clear one. The advantages of this can be two-fold. Firstly, an advantage of printing with a coloured binder, orange for instance, would be an overall effect of harmonized colour. Secondly, a particular colour could be chosen for the binder, in order to fit in with the theme. With figures, for instance, an ochre, or burnt sienna, could be of use, whereas a light bluish-grey may well be chosen for a landscape subject.

In using a coloured binder, as opposed to a clear one,

resulting prints are likely to gain in unity. The entire surface area will take on the colour of the binder. The edges of the design will always be defined by the binder colour, even when areas of colour in the image have been worn out and do not print. If a particular design requires areas to be left plain, the remedy is simple: by using harder wax crayons, shapes coloured in will resist the binder and remain unprinted. Such crayons are sold as children's colouring sets, though a sharpened candle will equally serve this purpose. Being harder, they will not dissolve so readily with the binder, but act as a resist, leaving shapes and textures of unprinted paper.

Unexpected results and overprinting

Although the method of oil pastel prints is very direct, the results are, nevertheless, anything but predictable. One can at best only guess at the final outcome. Results are a matter of trial and error, yet the subtleties of texture and colour obtainable certainly seem to compensate for this. Apart from strengthening the image during printing, as already described, it is possible to overprint impressions that are too light, or have failed to print overall. With more pigment added to the screen, it should be possible to line up the edges of the print

through the screen and reprint the copy.

CONTÉ CRAYONS, CHARCOAL, AND SOFT COLOURED PENCILS

Apart from using oil pastels, it is worth while experimenting with other products that can be used in a similar way. Soft grades of conté crayon can be used to good effect, especially in combination with toned, or coloured binder. For designs that have more to do with drawing than colour, they can be easier to handle. Even charcoal, in combination with conté, can add a subtle range of greys.

Certain coloured pencils can also be used. The only answer as to what will work is to trial test anything that you think might remotely work. Use a small screen and trial print the various crayons and pencils, discarding those that fail to print.

READY-MADE STENCILS AND THEIR USES

'Ready-mades', as the name suggests, are items already in existence: items that do not have to be made, but can be printed from in their found state. In the case of screen printing, this could include any materials that are both flat and thin enough to be used as stencils.

The use of ready-made

stencils is by no means a new departure in print-making. Since the earliest of times, people have used natural found objects as stencils from which to print. In those days patterns were made by dabbing natural stains and pigments over the backs of leaves. Today, despite the use of modern tools and equipment, the principles involved are not dissimilar.

Natural forms

Natural forms suitable for stencils can provide a varied array of shapes and patterns. The variety of leaf patterns alone offers a good source of material. Add to this the different grasses, reeds and ferns around us, and one begins to appreciate the growing possibilities. Other forms, like flowers, the centres of which are too thick to use, can be flattened in a flower press before use.

Combinations of leaves etc. can be effectively used, either decoratively to create patterns, or in a picture-making sense to build up fantasy landscapes. In both cases it pays to collect, before starting, an assortment of contrasting sizes and shapes.

Creating a fantasy landscape using leaves

For print size, use the previously-mentioned format of 40cm (16in) square. Mark out a 40cm (16in) square on cartridge paper on which to arrange the leaf stencils. Cut a 5cm (2in) circle out of newspaper to symbolize a sun or moon. Place the circle in the upper part of the marked-out square. Then, place a pattern of closely-positioned leaf shapes in the bottom third of the shape. Mix up two or three contrasting sky colours, and print this first image in the form of a blend.

When dry, tear or cut simple bush shapes from a sheet of newspaper, and position them to overprint on the lower part of the format. Place this over the first marked-out print, in printing order, and arrange patterns of small leaves within the torn-out shapes. Print this second image in a contrasting colour. Continue to print other overlapping shapes, containing negative leaf patterns, in different colours. After three or four printings the subtleties of the overprintings should add a sense of depth and interest to the overall imagery. Further variety can be added to the design by overprinting such things as branches previously cut from newsprint.

Trial runs and coloured backgrounds

Apart from items already mentioned, all sorts of bits and pieces can be tried out as stencils. But how well they will work, or what the patterns they produce will really look like, can only be guessed at. To test

their worth, they must first be printed. Making simple test prints of each item can provide the answer. Odds and ends – from feathers to lichens, seed heads to wood shavings – can be placed under a screen and printed in groups to act as reference. With small shapes, like seed heads, it may pay to thicken the ink to ensure they remain stuck to the screen. Also, it is worth bearing in mind that ready-made stencils, printed on a white ground, will produce a negative image surrounded by colour. This can be overcome by printing on toned or coloured paper, using white or light-coloured ink. The effect produced – a dark image, paper coloured, on a light ground – should add substance and a sense of solidity to the design.

Synthetic and manufactured materials: patterns and texture

The odds and ends of manufactured, or synthetic, origin that can be used as stencils to make patterns and textures are as plentiful as their natural counterparts. Thin plastics, metal foils, synthetic fibres and fabrics, to mention a few, are simple to come by. Perhaps the most obvious and easily usable ready-made stencils can be found in the wide variety of lace oddments available. Hand-made lace, with wonderful patterns that have

been badly torn or damaged, can sometimes be obtained, for the price of a few pence, at rummage sales. Bought new, ample variety of pattern can be found in the cheap form of machine-made lace. Similar patterns can be found in the imitation lace-style of paper or plastic doillies. Made from a single perforated sheet, doilies form excellent stencils.

Pieces of lace and paper doilies are most useful and can be used to good effect with paper stencils. They can be cut up and used in a variety of ways, such as introducing pattern and texture to parts of designs. They work especially well in representing patterns on clothes and fabrics. Even on their own, they make decorative enough patterns to go on greetings cards and posters. Other items can likewise be used to provide contrasting areas of texture in designs. Cotton waste and open weave patches of various materials can be printed in areas to help to liven up and relieve the monotony of otherwise flat designs.

PRINTING ON FABRICS

In the main, the procedure for designing and printing on fabric differs very little from printing on paper. The method of printing is the same as that already described for printing on paper; however, to be successful you will need to take into account some of the different properties of fabrics, as opposed to paper. In addition to this, the use that the fabric printing will be put to will also need to be considered. Outlined below are some differences and requirements that need to be borne in mind.

Fabrics (*Fig. 19*)

Cotton- or linen-based fabrics are ideally suited for printing bases. Made from natural fibres, they are resilient and will readily accept printing inks. Furthermore, they are easily washable and, providing they have been properly printed, should not present problems, such as ink peeling off during washing.

An inexpensive and easily-available form of cotton, unbleached calico, can readily be used as an all-round basic material on which to print. Suitable for most requirements, from printed wall-hangings to curtains, tablemats to tablecloths, calico is easy to work with.

Once you have gained some experience, and if you wish to try printing more refined or detailed images, natural silk is by far the best material to work on. Although the cost of silk can be prohibitive, it is sometimes possible to buy cheap remnants, or find secondhand silk items that can

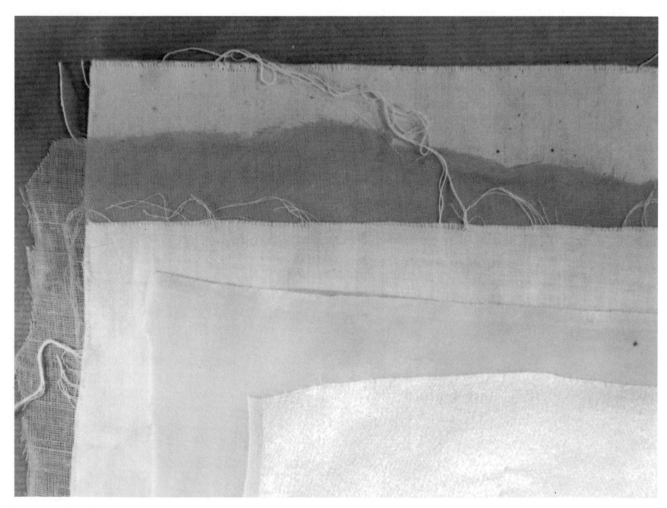

19   *A variety of printing fabrics*

be re–utilized for printing on. Failing this, there are numerous makes of cheap, thin materials, both cotton- and synthetic-based, meant to imitate silk, that are available.

Apart from the materials mentioned, which are traditionally used, it should be possible to screen print adequately on the majority of fabrics. As you gain experience, you will find that certain images and designs work better on one kind of material than on others. Likewise, the final use that the material will serve will help partly to determine the thickness and quality of fabric used.

Coloured hessian, although coarsely woven, provides a good background for simple one-colour designs to be used for items such as tablemats, shopping bags and wall-hangings.

The weave

In comparison with the smooth solid surface of paper, the textural open surface of fabrics (a result of the woven structure) limits to some extent what can be achieved. Whereas on paper almost any degree of detail, line and subtlety of colour can be contemplated, on material the same effects would be lost. When working with fabrics, it is better to create simple, clear-cut images.

Absorption

Another characteristic of fabrics is that the surface is more absorbent than that of paper. Whilst this is an advantage, in so far as the printing inks penetrate further into the fibres, making the image more durable and less susceptible to washing, a certain degree of clarity is nevertheless lost, due to the inks slightly spreading into the fibres. This provides one more reason for avoiding working in too detailed a manner.

Flexibility of fabrics

Unlike paper, cloth is highly flexible; before printing, it will need to be stretched and secured.

Preparing new fabrics

Most new materials will have been processed through a solution of starch, and stretched before being sold. This coating of starch, often referred to as the 'dressing', gives the appearance of fuller body to the fabric, and in combination with the stretching makes it more presentable. If printed on in this state, the colour would possibly fail to penetrate fully into the fibres, and may even rest on the surface only to peel off during the first wash.

To prepare new materials for printing, wash them thoroughly using a detergent to remove the dressing. Heavy cottons should be boiled. Finally, rinse the fabrics well and iron when dry.

Washable inks

For most purposes printed textiles will need to be cleaned or washed from time to time. To facilitate this, dyes, rather than ordinary pigments, are usually used for printing fabrics.

Dyes and binders

Home-made

A simple-to-use and inexpensive form of screen printing ink can be made from cold water dyes. Mixed with cellulose (wallpaper paste) binder, they not only work effectively, but are also stocked in a variety of shops.

To prepare for printing, first mix the cellulose paste as previously described for use on paper. Then, dissolve the cold water dyes and fixer using the smallest quantity of warm water necessary to do so. As a substitute fixer use four parts salt to one part soda. There are usually adequate instructions on fixers included with dyes. Too much water added to the dyes will produce the effect of overthinning when the dyes are added to the cellulose base. If this does happen, mix in more cellulose granules, stir thoroughly from time to time and leave for a while, until the added granules have completely absorbed the excess liquid. After printing and when the colours have dried, carefully iron the printed areas using a hot iron.

Manutex is a product derived

from seaweed and supplied by screen printing stockists for use with water-based inks and dyes. It can be prepared in a similar way to cellulose paste and provides a good economic binder.

Helizarin dyes and binders
Helizarin dyes and binders are specially manufactured for use in screen printing onto fabrics. Although more expensive than the above home-brewed concoctions, they are nevertheless moderately priced and good value for money. Ideally suited to fabric printing, they are both easy to use and simple to prepare: it is only a matter of adding the dyes to the binder in the required

proportions and stirring in well. The binder itself is sold in a ready-to-use state. Helizarin dyes, comprising a range of fifteen colours, can be obtained, as can the binder, from most silk screen suppliers. Fix the colours when dry by ironing with a hot iron, or bake at 140°C (284°F) for 5 minutes.

Dyed and tie-dyed backgrounds
The results of printing on a plain white background, depending on the design, can at times appear to look somewhat stark and clumsy. Small printing errors and slight differences in registration have a tendency to show up and even to appear magnified against the contrast

of a white background, whereas against a toned, or coloured, ground the same small discrepancies would be barely noticeable. In general, it is easier to print on a light-coloured material. Buying one or two cheap lengths of light-coloured fabric, or coloured remnants, can be a practical way of starting, but, with experience, dyeing your own material, using cold water dyes, will provide you with more options as far as subtlety of colour and tone are concerned.

In contrast to the natural flat colours so distinguishable in screen printing, the soft effects of tie-dyed backgrounds can act as an interesting foil. Another advantage is that tie-dye

20   *Simple motifs made from cut-away square shapes and based on the idea of birds and flight*

patterns can be produced quickly and easily. It can simply be a matter of screwing up handfuls of materials and tightly binding on bands of string or tightly-stretched thick rubber bands. The material is then immersed in a solution of cold water dye for a minute or so, then removed and hung up to dry. Once the string is removed, soft gradated patterns can be seen in the previously-tied places where the dye has not thoroughly penetrated the material, the tones and effects of which can provide a pleasing ground on which to print. Light-coloured tie-dye designs can particularly add to and enrich motifs printed in only one colour.

Repeat patterns
A motif printed a number of times on a length of fabric is called a 'repeat' (*Fig. 21*). Often several different images are used in the one design and made to repeat in a simple sequence. Perhaps the most interesting advantage of repeat printing is that the simplest and most mundane of motifs can take on a new significance when printed a number of times. With large lengths of fabric, it is not always practical, or desirable, to print the entire area. The aggregate effect of a number of repeats, printed in the form of a panel, or border, can be quite surprising. Likewise, the intervening spaces

21   *Examples of repeat patterns*

22   *A counterchange design, with parts of the motif dark against a light background, and parts light against a dark background*

23   *Both the negative and positive parts of the stencil have been used. A cut-out box shape from newsprint was placed around the cut-out bird to contain the printed background*

between images, especially when they are printed close to each other, can read as interesting shapes and accumulatively as unexpected overall pattern.

With the use of one small motif, a variable range of pattern can be built up, simply by changing the order of the repeat printing (*Fig. 21*). Apart from those illustrated, there are numerous grids that you can find to use. Before making a final choice, try printing a few patterns on newspaper, in order to get some idea of how the outcome will look on the finished length. Once a particular sequence of printing has been decided upon, guide lines and position marks can be lightly drawn on the cloth, prior to printing, using a soft pencil, or chalk.

Borders and panels
Printing borders or panels on large items, such as curtains, bedspreads and tablecloths, can often look more effective and less tiresome than printing the fabric throughout. If the right balance is struck between borders and background, the printed areas can form a pleasing contrast to the surrounding plain material, and the overall result will look all the better for it. For the best results try to keep the printed areas and background of different proportions. A ratio in the region of one-third border to two-thirds background should work well.

Simple designs: one-colour motif
To start with, it is easier to design a single motif and repeat print it in one colour. To give the appearance of added colour, use a fabric with a light-coloured background.

Paper stencils are the easiest method to experiment with initially. They can be drawn on newspaper, or layout paper, quickly cut out, then test printed a few times onto newspaper to see the effects of the repeat printing. Once you have decided on the design to be used and the sequence of printing, unless you have already stretched your material and intend printing immediately, it is better to cut another stencil. Trying to reprint with an already-used stencil is rarely successful, usually leading to all sorts of problems.

As a cautionary note, try to find an image with a strong shape to start with. Without the back-up of extra colours, the shape of the image is more significant. The weakness of a poorly designed and cut stencil will seem accentuated, whereas a strong shape, with variety of outline, will look none the worse for the absence of extra colours. In designing the image, look for a powerful silhouette, at the same time keeping it chunky and not too overworked or fussy. In doing

25   *Printing alternate images upside down*

26   *The same motif printed with a quarter turn each time*

this, it is sometimes more profitable to sketch out a number of different images to choose from, than to spend considerable time trying to improve on the first one or two drawn shapes.

Counterchange
When a design alternates in such a way that part of it appears dark against a light background, whilst the remaining parts appear light against a dark ground, the result is called a 'counterchange' (*Fig. 22*). This exchanging of tones is most useful in designing one-colour motifs, as it makes the best possible use of light and dark tone, seeming to add a further dimension. Worthwhile results can be obtained by using a counterchange of the same image. To achieve this, carefully cut out the image, retaining

24   *Small cut-out shapes of newsprint placed within a stencil can achieve an effect of counterchange.*

both parts. From a separate sheet of newspaper, cut out a box shape, slightly larger in proportion than the cut-out image. This will contain the printed background of the negative image. These stencils will enable you to print both a light and dark alternative version of the image (*Fig. 23*).

Apart from designing a fully-counterchanged design, leaving unprinted small shapes within the printed image can add variety and vigour to the overall design (*Fig. 24*). This can be done by cutting small shapes from newspaper and placing them inside the cut-out shape of the main stencil, prior to printing; they will stick to the mesh in the same way as the main stencil during the first

printing. With each printing you either have the opportunity to peel them off and reposition them, or to use others.

Once you are satisfied with the motif, think in terms of the various ways in which it can be printed. By experimenting on newspaper, you may find that instead of printing the image the same way up all the time, it will improve the overall result by printing every second image upside down (*Fig. 25*), or perhaps the motif might look better printed with a quarter turn each time (*Fig. 26*). Either way, it is always worth while spending time in deciding the best positioning and sequence of printing for a particular image.

27   *Printing a blocked colour shape over the entire image, or part of it (as illustrated by the lined area) is a simple way of introducing a second colour into a design. It does not require accurate registration, and is particularly useful when printing on white fabric*

Motif combined with simple colour blocks

An easy way of producing more colour, without the worry of incompatibility, is to print a motif in combination with simple colour blocks. This is simply achieved by repeat printing a square, or block of colour, over the area to be printed; when dry, the motif can be overprinted (*Fig. 27*). It is preferable, in design terms, to think of the colour blocks as harmonizing with the tone of the fabric – these simple shapes acting, in duality, as secondary background colour. In this way, the added colour will enhance the overall design, without the risk of confusing the end result, when the motif is finally printed in a contrasting tone or colour.

Securing the fabric for printing

Before printing, the fabric will need to be stretched and secured. At the same time, and because of the flexible nature of the material, it is advisable to pad out the printing surface with newspaper to take up any unevenness during printing.

A flat wooden table makes an ideal printing base. Failing this, a large drawing board, or piece of chipboard etc., will do just as well. Cover the printing base with a few layers of newspaper. Carefully position the fabric over this. Then, stretch the fabric evenly over the base, securing it as you do so with drawing pins around the edges.

Once this has been established, lightly indicate, using a soft pencil or chalk, the positioning for the particular sequence of printing to be used. For instance, if the image is to be repeated in rows, mark out the base lines and, with a series of dots along these lines, mark where each image is to be printed.

Procedure for printing

The actual printing technique is the same as that already described for printing on paper. Differences that do exist lie more in the nature of the printing. Instead of dealing with a single image at a time, as with paper, fabric printing involves repeat printing that can, according to its purpose, spread over considerable areas of fabric. One problem often encountered is that of freshly-printed images smudging. To avoid this, it is worth while placing clean newspaper over freshly-printed areas, especially on edges of the image that will be overlapped by the frame on the following printing. This also avoids picking up wet ink on the back of the frame during printing.

Once you have printed the first area of material that has been stretched and pinned down, place the inks and squeegee to one side and remove the drawing pins from the edges of the material. Then, carefully pull the printed material over the edge of the table, taking care not to smudge it, to rest on chair backs, and secure the next portion of fabric to be printed. The occasional small spot missed in printing can be spotted in using a brush. For best results, carry out any necessary retouching before the ink has dried.

Carefully hang up the printed material once the ink has set and leave to dry for two days. Before ironing, cover the printed areas with fresh newspaper. Allow a period of one week to enable the ink to harden thoroughly onto the fabric before washing.

Specializing in fabric printing

If your interests develop more towards fabric printing, it will pay you to improve your printing system towards that end. A padded printing surface is the first priority. This can be made by stretching a blanket

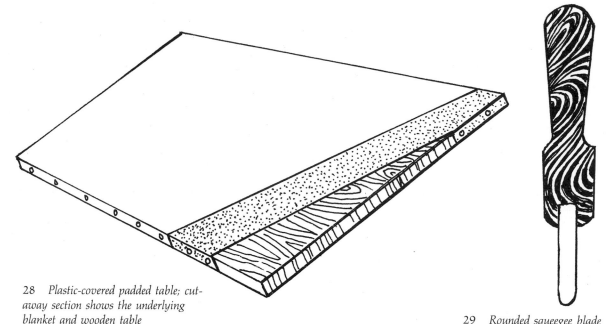

28   *Plastic-covered padded table; cut-away section shows the underlying blanket and wooden table*

29   *Rounded squeegee blade*

over a flat wooden table and securing it round the sides with either drawing pins or a staple gun. Over this, secure a covering of PVC-coated cloth, pinned around the sides of the table in the same way (*Fig. 28*). Make sure that both blanket and plastic covering are properly stretched out, so as to achieve a flat padded surface without wrinkles. The end result will give you a good support for printing fabrics. Unlike newspaper for padding, it will not tend to move around during printing.

Rounded squeegee blade
A further advantage can be gained from using a rounded squeegee blade (*Fig. 29*). The rounded edge of the blade enables more ink to be forced through the screen mesh. The resulting thicker deposit of ink has the advantage of offsetting the loss caused by ink soaking into the fabric.

Printex dyes and binder
As an alternative binder and dye for fabric printing, Printex is reasonably priced and simple to use. Like Helizarin, it is

marketed in a wide range of colours. The binder can be obtained in various sizes.

AVOIDING PROBLEMS

In the main, screen printing is a simple and straightforward process, and one that has benefited, during recent years, from the many improvements brought about by advances in modern technology. Although these steps forward have been achieved for the benefit of commercial printing, they are just as readily available to the fine art studio printer and amateur printer alike. During this time, refinements to inks and binders, improved screen meshes and improvements in the sphere of the photo positive process have ironed out many difficulties and hazards previously encountered.

So, what can go wrong? The answer is that even with a well-designed system and a careful approach, the occasional problem is still likely to occur from time to time. Unfortunately, one small mistake or oversight, can, if left unattended, spoil a print-run. The obvious solution is to

anticipate any mishaps before they occur and so avoid them. Failing this, one needs to quickly identify the reason for it happening. Once the cause has been identified, a remedy can be found, hopefully before too much damage has been done.

An important factor is to learn from past mistakes, so that they are not repeated. I still remember the time when, using a slightly dried-up orange tinter in a sky blend, I failed to mix it adequately before adding it to the other inks and binder. Even after cleaning the screen and thoroughly remixing the colour twice, the occasional pin prick of pure orange streaked across the sky during printing. The lesson, on that occasion, was to use only good colours and then thoroughly mix, with thinners, any that look even slightly dubious, testing them before adding them to the binder.

Finding the cause of problems
Finding the exact cause of a problem is not always easy. At times, a number of quite different factors can

accumulatively cause a mistake. If, for instance, small errors of register have been made in the cutting of stencils, a loose screen fabric, or loose hinges, would tend to magnify the discrepancy during printing. Once a problem has arisen, it is a question of looking at all the possible causes and identifying those responsible. Knowing what to look for when sorting out problems comes with experience. In the meantime, the following fault-finding and remedial suggestions should help you to overcome the most usual problems.

PROBLEM: registration out of alignment

Colours print with double image, or gaps appear between different colours.

CAUSE	REMEDY
(a) Screen fabric too loose.	Always check the screen tension before use. If it is loose, tighten it by using a staple gun, or drawing pins.
(b) Loose screen hinges.	Check movement on hinges. Tighten screws if necessary.
(c) Poorly cut or designed stencils.	If sufficient care has not been taken in the design and making of the stencils, the print will not work. If this occurs, the only remedy is to start again.
(d) Sharp change of atmosphere affecting printing stock.	If the atmosphere of the printing area radically changes during printing, the effect could cause the printing stock to swell, or shrink. Either way would affect the registration. Using fan heaters to hasten drying between printings could cause this. For the same reason, stack paper for printing in the area to be used for a few days prior to printing, to acclimatize it to the atmosphere.
(e) Loose register tabs.	If the register tabs become loose, they will need to be retaped down. Always ensure that paper is placed full against register guides.

PROBLEM: uneven colour

Colours appear weaker on certain parts of the print.

CAUSE	REMEDY
(a) Uneven pressure on the squeegee.	Apply even pressure to squeegee when printing.
(b) Squeegee blade has become rigid.	After periods of disuse, or in cold weather, polyurethane squeegee blades tend to harden. To counteract this, hold the blade in front of a fan heater, or run hot water over the blade. Then carefully massage the side of the blade to make it more flexible.

PROBLEM: pinheads of unwanted colour

CAUSE	REMEDY
Small breaks in stencil.	Raise the screen and patch the affected area with tape.

PROBLEM: ink seeps past the stencil edge during printing

This is more likely to happen when using paper stencils.
In all cases, carefully wipe the overlapping ink from the back of the stencil.

CAUSE	REMEDY
(a) Ink too thin.	Thicken mixture by adding more binder and pigments.
(b) Screen fabric too loose.	Paper stencils may not stick evenly to mesh, causing the stencil to ripple. Remove the stencil and tighten the screen fabric.
(c) Damp paper stencil.	Damp stencils may cause ink to seep through and overrun. Cut a new stencil.
(d) Torn stencil.	Mend small tears with tape. Failing this, cut a new stencil.

PROBLEM: paper stencil becomes unattached during printing

CAUSE	REMEDY
(a) Printing on damp ink.	If the print is still tacky when overprinting, the stencil may stick to the print, pulling away from the screen. Ensure that prints are dry before overprinting.
(b) Too large a surround on paper stencils.	If the surround on the paper stencil overlaps the taped border by too much, the edges of the stencil will flop down, pulling the stencil away from the screen. If this happens, cut back the overlapping stencil.
(c) Too slight, or uneven pressure put on squeegee during the first pull.	Carefully peel off the part of the stencil that has stuck down and reposition it on a fresh sheet of paper. Take another pull, this time using more, all-over, pressure.

PROBLEM: the screen clogs during printing

Printing becomes lighter and parts of the stencil cease to print.
Details become lost and blurred and the problem usually gets worse.

CAUSE	REMEDY
(a) Too little pressure on the squeegee.	Harder pressure on the squeegee should be tried and will work provided that the ink has not dried in.
(b) Ink is too thick.	Clean the screen and add the appropriate thinner to the ink and stir well.
(c) Ink dries in screen.	Small areas of drying-in can often be cleared by rubbing the area with a cloth soaked in the appropriate thinner. For large areas, especially when paper stencils are used, cut a new stencil, clean the screen and start afresh. To deter ink from drying in, always reflood the screen once a print has been taken.
(d) Printing stock is very absorbent.	If the paper is very absorbent, the ink may need to be thinned to compensate for this.

PROBLEM: blended colours appear streaky

CAUSE	REMEDY
(a) Colours insufficiently mixed on the screen.	Clean the screen and, with the edge of the blade, blend the colours in more fully.
(b) Colours in the blend consist of different thicknesses.	It is important that colours used in a blend are thinned by the same amount. If this is not done, colours may not blend evenly. To remedy this, clean the screen and remix colours, thinning to equal consistency.

2 REGISTRATION AND IMPROVING YOUR SYSTEM

Having dealt so far with the making of screens etc. and the basic printing technique, it is now possible to think in terms of improving your system. This can be done cheaply and without too much bother. The first priority is to attach the screen to a printing base. Doing this will ensure that the frame does not move during printing and so avoid spoiling prints. The second advantage of securing the frame in a fixed printing position is that an exact, repeatable registration of various stencils and colours can be obtained.

HINGED FRAME AND BASEBOARD

Baseboard

The baseboard over which the frame will fit needs to be perfectly flat and smooth. Thick plywood, or chipboard, is suitable for this purpose. Ideally, this should be covered with a layer of white formica. Either nail the formica cover to the base, pinning around the edges, or stick with impact adhesive. Easier still, buy the wood already laminated. Most DIY shops, catering for kitchen refurbishing, stock various laminated work tops. The purpose of the formica covering is to obtain a perfectly smooth surface that marks will show up on, that can easily be wiped clean, and that will readily carry the stuck-on register tabs necessary for the accurate alignment of stencils.

The size of the baseboard needs to be a few inches larger all round than the frame. For a frame of 60 × 60cm (24 × 24in) as suggested earlier, use a baseboard of 75 × 75cm (30 × 30in).

Hingebar and snap adjustment

Although the frame is often hinged directly to the baseboard (*Fig. 30*), the inclusion of a hingebar (*Fig. 31*) is a useful addition. The purpose of a hingebar is to allow for an adjustable raising and lowering of the frame, in relation to the baseboard (*Fig. 32*). This is done by either packing paper or card under the hingebar before tightening down, or adding metal washers

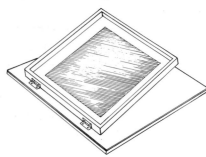

30 *Formica-topped baseboard with split pin hinges*

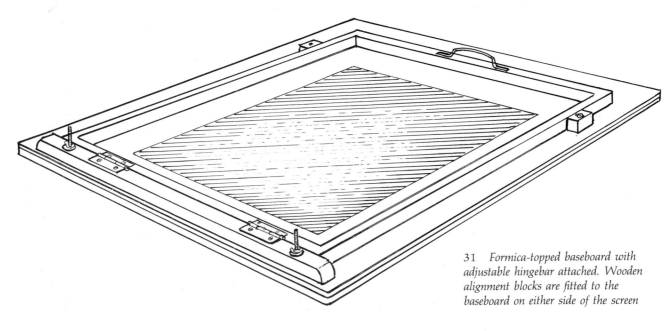

31 *Formica-topped baseboard with adjustable hingebar attached. Wooden alignment blocks are fitted to the baseboard on either side of the screen*

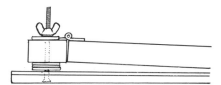

32   *The screen can be slightly raised and lowered from the baseboard by adding or taking away metal washers fixed to the hingebar. When using small screens, tape down card to the thickness of the washers used to the baseboard, to correspond to the front edge of the screen*

33   *During printing only the screen fabric directly beneath the leading edge of the squeegee blade is in contact with the paper. This diminishes the possibility of blurred results and runs*

to the bolts.

The benefits of a hinge bar are two-fold. Firstly, the height of the printing surface can be readjusted to cater for thick papers, card and even hardboard. Secondly, this adjustment can be used to create a gap between the printing surface and the mesh. This is called 'snap' or 'lift off'. The purpose of snap is to ensure that only that part of the screen that is being printed is in contact with the paper. As the squeegee is pulled across the screen, the printed areas of the screen progressively lift away from the print (*Fig. 33*). Only a moving line of contact, corresponding to the blade edge, is made with the print.

The degree of adjustment required will vary with the frame size. For a 60×60cm (24×24in) screen, adjust the gap on the hingebar to $\frac{1}{2}$cm ($\frac{3}{16}$in). Be careful not to over-adjust the clearance: a too-large gap could damage the screen, or place undue wear upon it.

When making the hingebar, its height should correspond to that of the frame. Use a 75cm (30in) long section of planed 5×5cm (2×2in) wood. This can be held in place across the top of the baseboard by two 6mm ($\frac{1}{4}$in) bolts and wing nuts. To do this, clamp the hingebar in the required position and drill a hole at either end. Use a 12mm ($\frac{1}{2}$in) bit to drill the holes at right angles through the hingebar and baseboard. It is essential that the holes should not exceed the bolt size, otherwise movement will take place during printing. The bolt heads should be countersunk into the back of the baseboard.

Hinges
For the purpose of cleaning and attaching certain types of stencils to the mesh, the frame will need to be easily removable from the base. It is also important that the frame, when replaced, goes back in exactly the same position. The easiest way of achieving this is to use two sets of push pin hinges (*Fig. 34*). These are similar to ordinary hinges, except that the centre pin

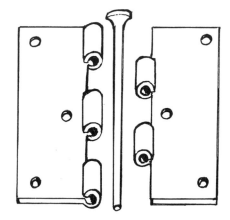

34   *Split pin hinges ensure that screens can be quickly and easily removed, or interchanged*

holding them together is removable. Either metal or nylon hinges are suitable.

When fixing, place the two sets of hinges a few inches in from either end of the screen, with both female hinges on the hingebar. Make sure they are in perfect alignment, then mark the screw holes. Use 2.5cm (1in) flat-headed screws. You will possibly need to drill 12mm ($\frac{1}{2}$in) holes, before screwing the hinges firmly in place. It is important that the hinges are truly aligned and the screws fit tightly, otherwise movement to the screen will occur.

When buying the hinges, it is advisable to get at least six sets of exactly the same size; 6.2cm ($2\frac{1}{2}$in) or 7.5cm (3in) sized hinges will be adequate. As these hinges would be identical, they can be used, with additional frames, in an interchangeable way. To do this, join two of the square male hinges to the existing female hinges on the hingebar. Place the new screen in position and mark out the screw holes. Secure the male hinges to the screen as before.

Alignment blocks

Even with the greatest amount of care taken in making a hinged baseboard, there is likely to be a small amount of movement present. To ensure that the frame returns to the exact printing position, alignment blocks can be used. These can be made from small pieces of wood (*Fig. 35*), and are slid into position and secured to the baseboard on either side of the frame (*see Fig. 31*) with screws and washers. To allow for adjustment, drill three holes, side by side, in each block. These can be filed down to form a slot, which will afford slight corrections to be made.

Prop or counterbalance

When removing prints, or

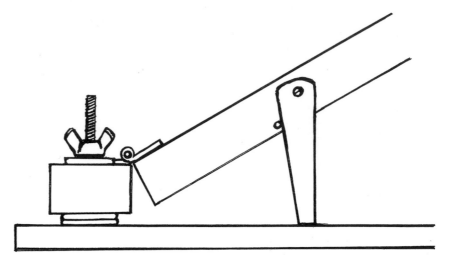

36   *Prop or leg – a simple device to keep the screen in a raised position*

replacing fresh paper, it is useful to have the screen remain in a raised position, so enabling one to have both hands free. This can be achieved in one of two ways.

Prop or leg

This is a simple device that can be made out of wood (*Fig. 36*) and screwed to one side of the frame. As the frame is raised, the leg drops into position, held in place by a small screw, or nail, sticking out from the side of the frame. To lower the screen again, the leg is moved, by hand, to a forward position.

Counterbalance

Although this method of keeping the frame in a raised position requires a little more planning, once operational it will work on its own (*Fig. 37*). To achieve this, secure a 60cm (24in) length of 5 × 2.5cm (2 × 1in) timber to the side of the baseboard, upright and in line with one side of the frame. Fasten a length of strong twine to the side of the frame, through a small pulley, or staple, at the top of the upright.

At the other end of the twine, tie iron or lead weights. Test the weights, by trial and error, so that they counterbalance the screen in a raised position.

USING AN IMPROVED SCREEN MESH

Good-quality cotton organdie is a useful screen fabric for starting with, as already described. Although it will not stand up to constant wear, it is relatively cheap and can easily be replaced. It is also well suited for experiments, simple cut-paper designs, and use with profilm and fabric printing. However, for printing on paper, requiring a thinner ink deposit, it has numerous disadvantages.

As your experience in screen printing grows, you will probably see the need for an improved screen mesh. This will enable you to cope more readily with issues such as sharper definition and close colour registration. Although the initial cost of a better fabric is higher, the improved mesh will be more resilient and stable, standing up to

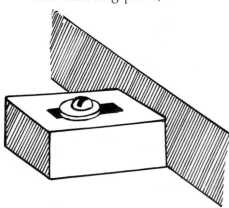

35   *Wooden alignment block*

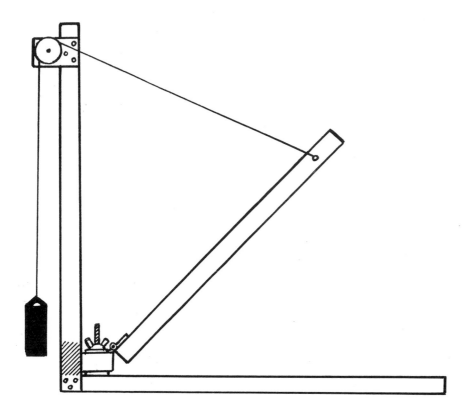

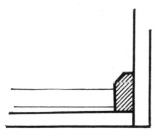

37   Screw and glue a wooden block to the upright, as illustrated. This will allow the counterbalance weight clearance, when attached to the pulley. For extra rigidity, glue a wooden block, as shown, to the bottom of the upright and the base

prolonged wear, cleaning and use.

Whereas silk was traditionally considered to be the best screen fabric, since the Sixties technological improvements within the industry have gradually replaced silk with a range of better synthetic screen fabrics. Silk is rarely used these days, although the process is still often referred to as 'silk screen' printing.

A good all-purpose screen fabric: monofilament polyester

When I started screen printing, three large screens came with the assortment of secondhand bought equipment. With little prior knowledge of screen meshes, apart from organdie, they seemed to work like magic. Extremely taut, the mesh had been mechanically stretched, and they worked well for everything. Over a period of time they were used for cut-paper stencils, tusche resist method, direct painting onto the screen and for photo stencils. Later on, when ordering more screens, I discovered they were monofilament polyester. The new screens were duly ordered from a handed-down written description; 'Monofilament Polyester 100 (centimetre) T Red'. Being more interested, at the time, in the practical possibilities of the medium than in the technicalities, this information sufficed for a considerable time. I still use the same screen mesh throughout. When ordering this screen mesh, be sure to quote the 100 as for centimetres, as both centimetre and inch mesh measurements are used.

If you do not intend using photo stencils, some expense can be saved. Monofiliment polyester 60 (centimetre) T mesh, although courser, is cheaper and equally suitable for methods of painting directly onto the screen and for cut stencils.

It is worth remembering that a high-quality screen mesh will only work to advantage if correctly stretched. Monofilament polyester is extremely rigid, stretches well and shows little sign of slackness, even after constant use. However, it does need to be stretched properly with the use of a stretching frame, or mechanical clamps. Screen printing suppliers usually have a mesh stretching service. For a slightly increased cost, they will stretch the mesh for you, on frames supplied by you, or new ones.

Whilst the above information should provide adequate advice on choosing an improved screen mesh, the following may help to explain some of the technicalities.

Multifilament and monofilament screen meshes

The thread from which screen printing fabric is woven can be classified under two main headings: multifilament and monofilament. Multifilament thread, as the name implies, is a thread spun from a number of separate strands, whereas, monofilament thread comprises one thick welded strand. Highly magnified, the difference between the two types of thread becomes more obvious (*Fig. 38*).

The multifilament thread magnified resembles the uneven structure of rope. This unevenness allows deposits of ink to build up in frayed and worn threads, affecting the printing potential and making screen cleaning difficult. Added to this, the rough texture restricts the use of very fine weaves, making detailed printing difficult.

Monofilament thread magnified has a smoother, less-interrupted finish. It can be woven to a finer tolerance, essential for fine detail printing. Less likely to fray, it is stronger and will stand up to greater use and wear. Ink is less likely to build up in the mesh and screen cleaning is easier. Organic-based threads, such as cotton organdie and silk, are multifilament, whilst synthetic threads, like nylon and polyester, can be either multifilament or monofilament.

38   *Multifilament mesh*

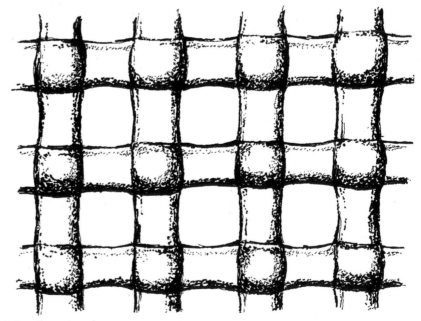

Monofilament mesh

Synthetic screen fabrics: nylon and polyester

Both nylon and polyester screen fabrics are available these days, mainly in the form of monofilament mesh. Whilst the low cost of nylon mesh may seem attractive, it has many disadvantages when compared to polyester, the most important of which are it that lacks stability and is less rigid than polyester. This tendency makes it unsuitable for work requiring closely-registered colours.

Monofilament polyester bolting cloth

At present, monofilament polyester mesh is generally considered to be the best screen printing fabric available. It is more rigid than other meshes and has good stability. Its resistance to water, chemicals and to abrasion makes it easy to clean and highly durable. Monofilament polyester is very suitable for printing on paper: the general stability of the mesh provides an extremely rigid support for stencils, ensuring close colour registration. Finer meshes are used for carrying and printing detail of minute size.

Different grades of screen mesh

With synthetic screen fabrics, the grade of the mesh is usually indicated by a letter placed after the mesh count. The letter is used to describe the thickness of the threads used in the weave: S means light, M medium, T heavy, and HD extra-heavy duty. The letters are sometimes qualified by such terms as 'standard weight', indicating that the measurement

is of general standard and does not merely relate to a particular manufacturer's range of products.

Mesh number: quality of the weave (synthetic meshes)

The coarseness or fineness of the weave is defined by the number of threads to the centimetre or inch. Low thread numbers indicate a coarse, more open weave mesh; high thread numbers specify a much finer woven mesh, capable of carrying more detailed and intricate stencils. Thread counts vary from about 30 per centimetre to well over 100 per

centimetre. For instance, meshes of 120 are used mainly for half-tone printing. Open weave, low number, meshes are cheaper in price than finely woven ones. However, coarser meshes cannot be used for the same diversity of work.

As an approximate guide to different mesh uses, a mesh of 40 per centimetre is suitable for hand-cut stencils. For methods using direct painting onto the screen, use a 60 per centimetre mesh. Photo stencils will require a mesh of 100 per centimetre. The chart below can be used as a quick guide to different mesh uses.

Monofilament polyester mesh count in centimetres	Uses	Printing characteristics
40	Hand-cut stencils	Prints with a thicker deposit of ink
60	Hand-cut stencils Direct painting onto the screen Tusche resist method	Moderately fine detail possible
100	Hand-cut stencils Direct painting onto the screen Tusche resist method Photo stencils	Copes with fine detail Best all-purpose mesh Leaves a thinner ink deposit
120	Half-tone printing	Minute detail possible Very fine ink deposit Mesh tends to clog up easily, due to the size of mesh openings. Requires thinner inks

Red and orange mesh

Synthetic mesh, such as polyester, is often marketed in a dyed form. The red or orange dye is added to prevent light scattering during direct photo stencil exposure, ensuring a more accurate stencil.

REGISTRATION AND OVERPRINTING

So far, either single-colour (monochrome) prints, or multi-colour designs, depending on shapes overprinted in contrast to underlying patterns of shapes, have been discussed. In neither case has there been a particular need for succeeding colours to be in agreement. It was more a process of building up a composite design, where the shapes on the first stencil were printed in opposition to those on the following ones. By doing so, a relatively quick and easy way of making prints, that relied on contrast as a point of interest, was established.

Yet, no matter how successful this method may appear, you will possibly reach a stage where this type of image-making will seem limited. Because it is a 'trial and error' way of doing things, there are no guarantees of success. Luck plays a role, and at times one may not be able to control this way of image-making with anything like 100 per cent success.

In expanding a range of new techniques, you will need to come to terms with registration. By 'registration' I mean the best positioning of stencil to paper, to ensure that each printed area corresponds precisely to the overall design, so that, when several stencils are printed, they are positioned in an exact way, enabling the combined result to be in agreement.

It is not only at the printing stage that care needs to be taken. At each stage in the process, from planning the design and working out a colour scheme, through to finished printing, the work will need to be synchronized. A clearly-defined design, closely-relating stencils, tight screen mesh, and carefully-positioned register guides will all influence the final result.

To achieve accurate registration you will need to use a hinged frame and baseboard. The screen, when lowered, will always come to rest in the same position on the baseboard. Any stencil on the screen will do likewise. By fixing simple register guides to the baseboard, one can also ensure that each sheet of paper to be printed can be placed in the same corresponding position to the design. With both the stencil and paper in fixed corresponding positions, it is possible to produce any number of prints with the various colours in agreement no matter how many times you repeat the process.

Pencilled crosses

To assist with an easy reassembly of the stencils, I often place a small pencilled cross in the centre of both the top and bottom margins of the key tracing. Before cutting each stencil, the two crosses are drawn in. When reassembling the stencils, to check for accuracy or see how colours overprint, the various crosses are soon lined up on a light box, or against a window.

Key drawing

It is essential to have a clearly-defined design. Once you are satisfied with the general appearance of your drawing, or colour design, tape a sheet of layout paper over the top. Then, using a fine-tipped pen or sharp pencil, carefully draw around the edges of the various shapes and contours of any colour separations. Also line in the four edges bordering the design. This key tracing can be used for cutting, or making, the various stencils required. It is also useful, when setting up the paper position, as a guide for registering the printing.

Making an accurate set of stencils

Because layout paper is semi-transparent, it is necessary to fix a sheet of cartridge paper to the board before taping down the key tracing. When cutting stencils, the key tracing also tends to get cut up. To prevent this, I often tape a sheet of clear acetate over the top for protection. With the key tracing in place, you can tape a second sheet of layout paper over this and proceed to cut the first stencil. As you proceed, it is a good idea to check the accuracy of registration. To do this, tape down the stencils over each other on a light box. The same effect can be produced by taping the stencils to a window pane; on an average day, the light should be sufficient to show through a number of paper stencils, indicating any discrepancies in the cutting.

Overlapping the colours

Whereas the function of registration is the accurate placing of colours in agreement with each other, there is no such thing as a finite state of accuracy. It is a relative term. Accuracy can only be achieved in varying degrees.

When cutting stencils for colours that butt against each other, it would be almost impossible to both cut and print the two stencils with the colours just touching all the way round. Both at the cutting and printing stage, small discrepancies are bound to occur, thus resulting in small gaps between the two colours. To overcome this, it is necessary to cut one of the stencils with a small overlap. A 1mm ($\frac{1}{16}$in) overlap is small enough, so as not to look crude

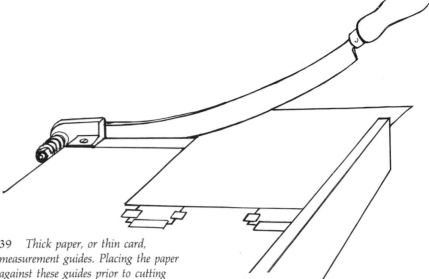

39   *Thick paper, or thin card, measurement guides. Placing the paper against these guides prior to cutting provides a degree of mechanical accuracy*

when printed, yet is sufficient to compensate for small mistakes in cutting and printing. It is advisable to apply this throughout, to any parts of a design where colours are to be printed side by side. For preference, overlap the stencil of the lightest or weakest colour. For example, where blue and orange are to be printed next to each other, overlap the orange stencil.

Cutting paper to size

Although not essential, a guillotine is very useful for cutting paper to size. Apart from cutting a straight edge, if used correctly, with the sheet levelled against the back edge, the paper will be squared up in the cutting process. It is always necessary, for the purpose of registration, to cut the paper square.

Failing the use of a guillotine, a steel straight edge, sharp craft knife, set square and a sheet of thick card as backing, are required. By piling them together, it should be possible to cut a few sheets of paper at a time. Always place the steel rule on the inside of the line to

be cut, cutting against the outer edge of the steel. In this way, if the knife deviates from the line you will not spoil the paper.

Paper guides for cutting paper
The quickest and most accurate way of cutting a number of sheets of paper using a guillotine is by using paper measurement markers (*Fig. 39*). These can be made from thick paper, or thin card. Cut out two small squares. Place the first sheet of paper on the guillotine, fully up against the back support, and adjust to the required cutting position. Then carefully tape down the paper squares against the edge of the paper. Cut the first sheet and feed in the second one to meet the measurement guides. If a second cut is needed, the guides can be pulled up and repositioned.

Register guides

A key factor in precision printing is the use of registration guides (*Fig. 40*). They provide a simple mechanical means of registering colours with accuracy. As long as the paper is fed into the

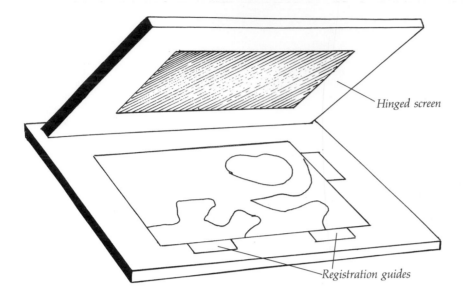

Hinged screen

Registration guides

40 *Simple taped-down paper, or thin card, registration guides*

guides correctly (an easy task) any number of facsimile prints can be obtained. The guides are easy to make, consisting of pieces of cut paper or thin card. It saves time to cut a good supply of them. Three are needed for each stencil to be printed. They can be made from 5cm (2in) wide guillotined strips of paper, cut up to about 7.5cm (3in) lengths. Unless you intend printing on very thin paper, it is preferable to cut them from a paper of similar thickness to your printing stock.

Master copy for keying in the design

Whether proofing or editioning a design, a sheet of paper, taken from the printing stock, needs to be kept aside as a master copy for keying in the image. On this sheet of paper, draw a line corresponding with the bottom edge of the image and another to correspond with the right-hand edge of the image

(*Fig. 41a*). Then place your key tracing over this. Carefully adjust the tracing until the right-hand side and bottom edge of the image are in agreement with the two lines (*b*). Tape the tracing down in this position. Cut a strip of thin card and tape it to the bottom border of your master copy (*c*). With this card extension, you can move the master copy into place when the screen is down.

For cut-paper stencil

For cut-paper stencils, the procedure is different and easier. Each paper stencil can be registered and stuck to the screen in one move. As each stencil is used, it is carefully positioned over the master copy, with the right-hand side

41a *Draw two lines*

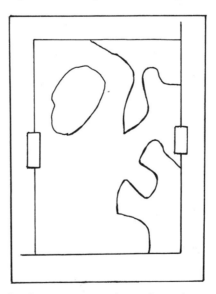

b *Align tracing over this, and tape down*

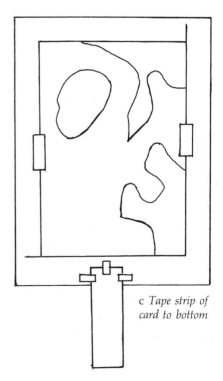

c *Tape strip of card to bottom*

and bottom edge in agreement with the drawn lines. The master copy is taped down to the baseboard. Then the screen is lowered and a print taken, with the stencil adhering to the screen. Before the first print is removed, the register guides should be taped in place. This procedure is repeated for each stencil used.

Lining up the image through the screen

The most widely used and simplest method of registration is 'through the screen'. The clarity of the key tracing should be sufficient to show up well through the clear parts of the screen. Place the master copy, with taped-on key tracing, on the baseboard and lower the screen. Use the card extension, which should extend out under the screen, to move the master copy. In this way, the master copy can be shifted around, under the screen, so that by looking through the screen from above, you can position it to correspond perfectly with the screen image.

It is important that, with each stencil, you use the same references for alignment. In this way you can keep to a consistent procedure, avoiding mistakes and confusion. The only parts of an image that remain constant throughout are the four edges. By always paying particular attention to lining up the right-hand side

and bottom edge of each stencil in turn, the rest of the image, provided the stencils have been made correctly, should be in agreement.

Printing procedure

Once the master copy is in alignment, carefully raise the screen and secure the copy to the baseboard with tape. Lower the screen once more and check the registration. Using outstretched fingers, you can press the screen down firmly against the paper. By doing so, a finer comparison can be made. Once satisfied, raise the screen, tape down two register guides against the bottom edge and one against the right-hand side of the paper (*see Fig. 39*). Remove the key tracing and print the master copy. With this removed, the next sheet of printing stock can be placed against the register guides, taped into place, and printed, and so on.

When printing a long run, stop from time to time to check for accuracy. You might find that small adjustments to the guides are needed. Slight stretching of the screen material, with use, could cause this. Also, the hinges may work slightly loose.

IMPROVED PRINTING INKS AND BINDERS

Whilst cellulose binder mixed with poster colour is the cheapest and easiest substance

to start with, in time you may find it limiting. As your design and printing capabilities improve, the need for better-quality inks and binders may seem more pressing.

In deciding on what type of inks and binder to use, various factors, including the working area, should be taken into consideration. For printing on paper, oil-based inks are very suitable and widely used. Yet, if you are using a room in your house to print in, especially a kitchen, they should be avoided: apart from being messier to work with, the inks, solvents and thinners are both toxic and flammable.

Emulsified binders

Emulsion-based binders are made from a mixture of oil and water. This is often in the form of white spirit and water. Being a strange hybrid of water- and oil-based systems, it is possible to mix either water-based colours or oil colours into it. Although it can be readily cleared from the screen with warm water, unlike simple water-based binders it will not wet and spoil paper stencils.

Helizarin binder

Helizarin binder type two, although specially produced for screen printing onto fabrics, can also be used very effectively as a base for printing onto paper. Widely available and moderately priced, it can be

42   *Helizarin binder*

with soap, or washing-up liquid, and gentle rubbing.

Source of colour

There is little point of improving the quality of the binder only to use inferior pigments. Whereas poster paints are quite suitable for use with cellulose binder, their permanence and staining power are somewhat limited.

Acrylic paints with Helizarin binder

Most makes of acrylic paint are of artist quality. Finely ground and of good colour saturation, they are obtainable in ranges of over thirty different colours. Although not designed for use in printing, they nevertheless make an excellent colouring source for use with Helizarin binder. Some makes are more fluid in substance than others, and due to this can be mixed more easily with the binder. Obtainable in relatively small tubes, they take up less room and are more economic to use than printing dyes that often come in sizeable tins.

The range of colours available makes colour matching and mixing an easy task. The fine consistency and pureness of colour means that a range can be created from delicate transparent shades to intense colours. Apart from primary and secondary colours, the range of earth colours, like ochres and oxides, can be of

obtained in three sizes: 1 litre, 5 litre and 20kg. For both amateur and professional artist alike, wishing to work to a high standard of printing, without the expense of setting up a specialized print room, it is an ideal product.

Emulsion-based, it has ample body, mixes well with water-based pigments and is easy to mix and wash from the screen. It can be used in the same way as ready-mixed cellulose binder, yet without the need to thicken, or dilute with water. Being of ample body, it is very suitable for use with paper stencils and organdie stretched screens. When in use, it possibly lasts longer than oil-based inks, before starting to dry into the screen. Any colour that does dry in can easily be removed with warm water. Persistent problem areas can be treated use. Readily available in acrylics, these colours can be difficult to create from printing dyes and inks, ranges of which sometimes consist of little more than primary colours. A further advantage of using acrylic colours can be gained at the design stage. Colour roughs can be worked out, using the same colours as those in the final printing. Although the printed colour will have a different quality to painted colour, the results will, nevertheless, be more compatible.

The drying times between printings are such that several colours can be overprinted in the course of a day. Using artist quality colours means that fine degrees of subtlety can be achieved through overprinting. Opaque colours can simply be obtained by adding white paint to the colour mix.

WORKING DIRECTLY ONTO THE SCREEN

The most straightforward way of making a stencil is to paint an image, using a screen filler medium, directly onto the screen. Painted-in areas will form the masked-out parts of the design, in the same way that paper does when using cut-paper stencils. In other words, you carefully paint around the image to make a negative blocked-out stencil. The untouched open areas of screen that are left will allow ink to pass through them to form the printed image.

Working directly onto the screen provides a far greater range of possible printed effects than those obtained by cut-paper stencils. Apart from solid areas of colour, all sorts of broken tones and textures can be produced. With different brushes, stippled, dry brush and splattered effects can be achieved. Items like sponges, crumpled cloth and corrugated cardboard can be used with screen filler medium to press textures onto the design.

Block-out mediums
Whereas a wide range of substances could be painted on the screen to form usable stencils, only those block-out mediums that can be dissolved after use are practical to work with.

Stencil glue
Stencil glue can be obtained from any screen printing suppliers. It should be fully water-soluble after use. If unsure about a particular brand, test it before use on a scrap of fabric. After completely drying, it should wash out easily with warm water. Glue stencils can be removed from the screen more readily than either lacquer, or shellac. Yet because glue stencils are water-soluble, they cannot be used with water-based inks.

The glue should be mixed to a thin cream-like consistency. If it is made too thin, it will shrink on drying out, leaving large pin holes in the stencil. On the other hand, if mixed too thick, it will be difficult to apply, going on unevenly. It might crack during the printing, breaking down the stencil. To adjust the mixture, add either more glue or water accordingly. Water-based colour can be added to the glue to make it contrast with the screen.

Lacquer
Lacquer stencils can be used with both water- and oil-based printing inks and are obtainable in a range of contrasting colours. The density of black lacquer makes it very suitable for use. If the mixture is too thick, add a modicum of lacquer thinner. Lacquer thinner, which is acetate-based, is also the solvent for removing stencils from the screen after use.

Shellac
Shellac stencils can also be used with water- and oil-based inks. The thinner and solvent to remove stencils is denatured alcohol. However, as the stencils are more difficult to remove completely from the screen than lacquer ones, they are not as practical to use.

Stencils that are well made, using glue, lacquer or shellac, stand up well to printed use. It should be possible to achieve editions of a few hundred copies from these stencils.

Method of working

1   Make a key tracing on a sheet of layout paper from the design.

2   Place the key tracing under the screen and draw the design onto the screen fabric.

3   Support the screen above the working surface. This is easily done by placing two lengths of 5 × 2.5cm (2 × 1in) timber under two opposite sides of the screen. Apart from raising the screen, this will provide a firm support.

4   Using glue, lacquer or shellac, paint in all the negative areas surrounding the design. Add any required textures, such as stippling, with brushes and sponges, etc. It is the areas that are not meant to print that should be blocked out. The untouched open areas of the screen will form the printed image.

5   Allow the painted stencil to dry thoroughly. The time this takes will depend on the medium used and the room temperature. A fan heater can be used to shorten the drying time of glue and shellac stencils, which take longer to dry than lacquer ones. When dry, hold the screen up to the light and check for pin holes. Spot these in with a brush.

Advantages of working on a sized screen

Glue stencils are so much easier to deal with than either lacquer or shellac stencils. They can be removed from the screen after use quickly, without using unpleasant solvents. Unfortunately, water-based inks are the only practical medium for many people, making glue stencils unsuitable.

One way round this problem is to size the screen with glue, before making lacquer or shellac stencils. Then, instead of filling the screen mesh, the lacquer or shellac attaches itself to the thin coating of glue size. When the painted stencil has dried, water is used to dissolve the thin coating of glue in the open areas of the stencil. When dry, the stencil can be printed using water-based inks.

The advantages of this method are twofold. Firstly, by washing the screen from the back, the glue size is easily removed, taking the lacquer or shellac stencil with it, thus avoiding the use of unpleasant solvents. Secondly, a stencil painted on a sized screen will be better defined, with sharper edges. This is because the stencil is painted on the smooth surface of glue, which bridges the mesh, instead of on the textural surface of the screen fabric.

Method of working on a sized screen

1   Mix the glue to a consistency of thin cream, using approximately one part glue to three parts water.

2   Using a card scraper, apply one coat of glue to the screen (*Fig. 43*). This should be done in the manner described for stencils (see tusche stencils, method of working). Try to keep the glue evenly spread, leaving a thin film across the screen.

3   Leave until the glue is completely dry. A fan heater can be used to speed the drying time.

4   Place the drawn design on a flat working surface, with the screen over the top. Paint in the design on the sized screen using lacquer or shellac (*Fig. 44*). The lacquer or shellac will form a coating over the glue size, but will not penetrate to the screen fabric.

5   Allow the painted stencil to dry completely.

6   Firmly support the screen, in a level position, above the working surface. Do this with two pieces of 5 × 2.5cm (2 × 1in) timber placed at two opposite ends of the screen.

7   Use a wet sponge to carefully wash over the top of the screen (*Fig. 45*). The water, while not affecting the lacquer or shellac stencil, will soften

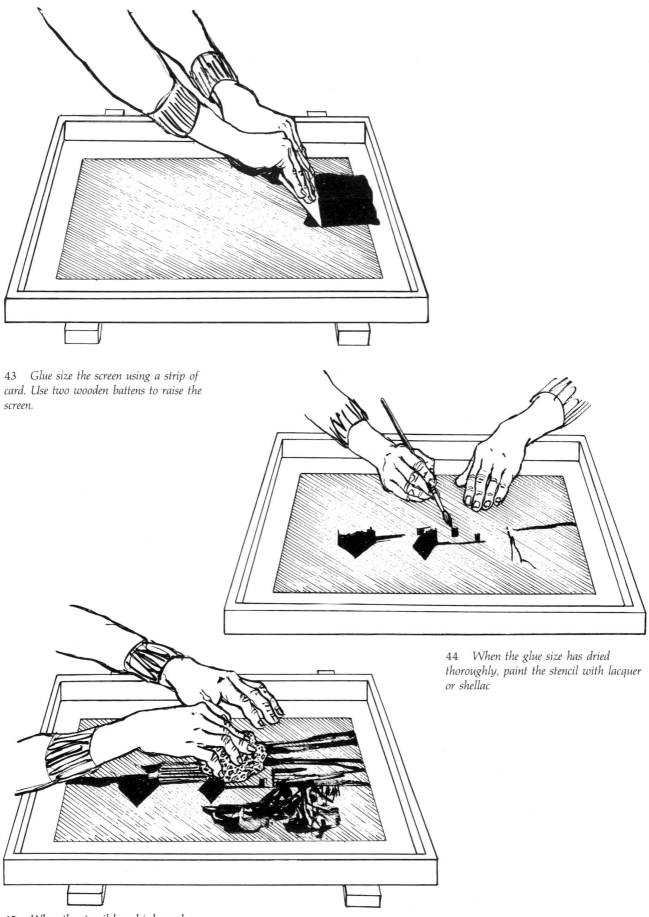

43   Glue size the screen using a strip of card. Use two wooden battens to raise the screen.

44   When the glue size has dried thoroughly, paint the stencil with lacquer or shellac

45   When the stencil has dried, wash out the open areas of the screen with a sponge and water

and dissolve the glue size in the open areas of the stencil. Use a minimum of water to remove the glue. If excess water is used, it can flood or seep under the painted parts of the stencil and damage the glue support, which would loosen and impair the stencil. For the same reason, keep the screen level throughout the process of removing the glue size.

8 Dry the top of the screen with a clean cloth, or paper towels. Thoroughly wipe over all open areas of the stencil to remove any traces of glue.

9 When you have completely removed all traces of glue from the open areas of the stencil, and the screen has dried, check the screen against the light for pin holes. These can be painted in with the same medium used on the stencil. When dry, the stencil is ready for printing.

KNIFE-CUT FILMS

Knife-cut films consist of thin sheets of film material that are lightly secured to supporting backing sheets. As the name infers, the films are used to make knife-cut stencils. To make a stencil, the areas intended to print are cut through to the backing sheet and then carefully peeled away from it, after which the film is adhered, by various means, to the mesh. As the films are moderately transparent, a tracing can be used as a guide when cutting the stencil.

Printed results from knife-cut films are not unlike those of paper stencils. Because the general definition of printing using knife-cut stencils is sharper, more detailed and intricate images can be made. The reasons for this are two-fold. Firstly, any number of free-standing, floating, areas can be used in a design, as they are kept in place on the backing sheet until they are secured to the screen. Secondly, knife-cut films are thinner and securely adhere to the screen mesh, unlike paper stencils which are merely held in place by the printing ink. There are three different types of knife-cut film available these days.

Iron-on, shellac-based

This is a knife-cut film which consists of a shellac film layer backed onto waxed paper. The film is secured to the screen mesh by using a warm iron. It is ideally suited for use with organdie and can be used with silk. However, it does not bond well to synthetic meshes and should not be used with either polyester or nylon screen fabrics. Shellac stencils are not affected by water and can therefore be used with water-based as well as oil inks. Due to this, shellac stencils are particularly useful for fabric printing. The film can usually be purchased by the sheet, or by the roll.

Procedure for using shellac film

1 Secure a master tracing of the design to a light box, or drawing board. Cut a piece of film slightly larger than the design, and, with the shellac film layer facing upwards, tape it over the tracing (*Fig. 46*).

2 Cut around the edges of the shapes to be printed (*Fig. 47*). Use enough pressure to cut right through the film coating, but do not cut through the backing sheet. Peel away the shapes of film from the areas of the stencils to be printed. When lifting these shapes, carefully prise the point of the knife under the edges of the film to gain a start. Ensure that you remove all unwanted parts of the film, leaving the areas to be printed thoroughly clear.

3 Spread a few sheets of newspaper on a flat working surface. Place the film on the paper, with the shellac stencil facing upwards. Position the screen over the film and lay a sheet of newspaper over the screen mesh. Use a domestic iron, set to the correct temperature for the material, to iron on the stencil. Before peeling off the backing sheet, wait for the material to cool thoroughly. After use, shellac stencils can be removed from the screen by using methylated spirits.

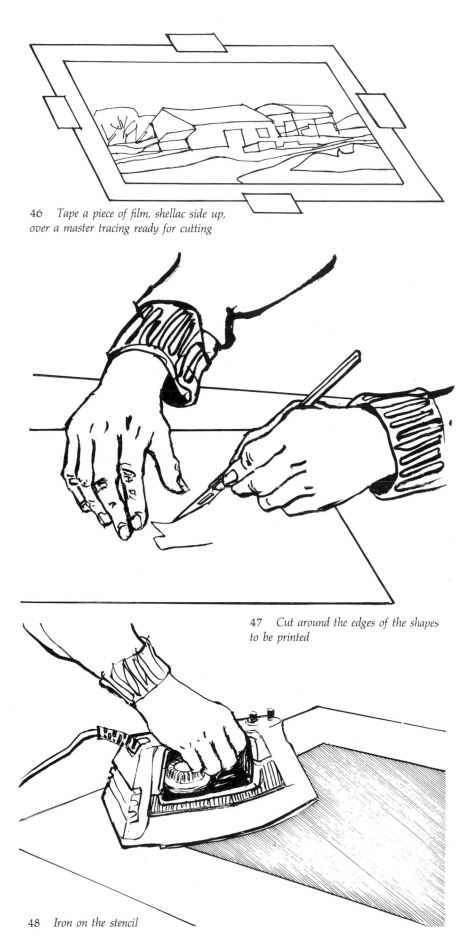

46 *Tape a piece of film, shellac side up, over a master tracing ready for cutting*

47 *Cut around the edges of the shapes to be printed*

48 *Iron on the stencil*

Water-based

Water-based knife-cut film usually consists of tissue paper impregnated with a water-soluble gum, backed onto a sheet of waxed paper. These films are ideally suited to use with polyester, nylon and terylene meshes, and can also be used with organdie and silk. They are the easiest to use type of knife-cut film, and the simplest to remove from the screen. The printed stencils have good definition. However, being water-based, these stencils cannot be used with water-based inks, unless reinforced with varnish.

Cutting and preparing water-based film is the same as for shellac film, until the stage of securing the stencil to the screen. Then water, instead of heat, is used to bond the stencil to the mesh. To adhere the film to the screen mesh, proceed as follows.

1 Firstly, ensure that the screen is thoroughly clean and has been properly degreased.

2 In order to provide good contact throughout between the film stencil and screen mesh, a support is needed. For this use a piece of mounting card or hardboard, larger than the film stencil and smaller than the screen frame. Bevel the edges and corners of the hardboard to prevent it snagging the screen. Place the support, with a sheet of newsprint over it, on a flat working surface. Over this, place the film stencil, stencil side upwards. Then, lower the screen onto the stencil (*Fig. 49*). If you need to position the screen accurately for registration, pencil in, on the screen, the four corners of the design beforehand, to act as placement guides.

3 Adhere the film stencil to the mesh with a sponge dampened with water. With a dabbing and wiping motion, continually work the sponge across the front of the screen, from one side of the stencil to the other (*Fig. 50*). As you progress, the colour of the stencil should darken. This will indicate how the procedure is progressing. It should enable you to dampen the stencil more evenly, to ensure an overall good adhesion to the mesh. In achieving this, do not make the sponge too wet: this would over-soften the gum stencil, weakening it and affecting the sharp edges. As soon as the stencil has been adequately dampened, it must be blotted with sheets of newspaper to soak up excess moisture. To assist the adhesion of the stencil to the mesh, sandwich it, by placing clean newspaper over the mesh, a piece of hardboard over this and a weight on top (*Fig. 51*). A fan heater can be used to assist the drying.

When thoroughly dry, the backing sheet can be carefully peeled away. Any resistance to

49   *Simplified cut-away diagram, showing the order from top to bottom: screen, film stencil, newsprint, hardboard, working top*

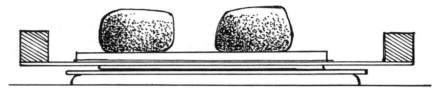

50   *Use weights to assist good stencil adhesion*

51   *Stick the stencil to the screen by dabbing with a damp sponge*

this would mean that the stencil has not thoroughly dried, in which case you should leave the stencil a while longer before attempting to lift the backing sheet again. When finished with, the stencil can easily be removed from the screen with water.

Lacquer-adhering
Lacquer-adhering films consist of a stencil film layer backed onto a sheet of paper, or

plastic. Red masking film is within this category, and it can be used either for knife-cut lacquer-type adhering stencils, or as cut positives for making photo stencils. The stencils are cut in the same way as shellac- or water-based ones. After this they are carefully secured to the mesh with an adhering fluid, which is usually lacquer thinner. But, to be certain, check with the supplier, to ensure that you use the correct adhering fluid for a particular film. Secure the stencil to the mesh as follows.

1 Position the screen over a support to ensure good stencil contact, in the same way as for water-based stencils.

2 To secure the stencil, use two pads of rag, one dry, the other soaked in adhering fluid and squeezed out. Dampen a small area in the centre of the stencil by dabbing with the wet cloth over the front of the screen mesh. Then quickly dry the area by rubbing quite hard with the dry cloth. The colour of the stencil will darken when the area has stuck securely to the mesh. Continue with the same procedure, working outwards towards the edges of the stencil, securing progressively smaller areas of stencil to the screen. Be careful not to over-dampen the stencil, as the adhering fluid is also used to remove stencils.

Once the stencil is complete, with the backing paper removed, the borders can be blocked out in the usual way, with screen filler compatible to the printing ink.

Knife-cut films are quite costly, although this hardly matters when working with small designs. With large designs, only intricate areas, or those requiring sharp edges, need be made using knife-cut film. Large simple areas of a design can simply be blocked out with a brush, using an appropriate screen filler.

A DIRECT POSITIVE IMAGE: TUSCHE RESIST

One difficulty of painting a stencil directly onto a screen is having to think in terms of making a negative image. From a design point of view, it is hard to visualize the open areas of screen as being the printed image. The parts blocked in with screen filler always appear more positive, as though *they* should be the areas printed.

There is, however, one direct method in which a positive image can be initially painted onto the screen: the 'tusche resist' method. This is a method of stencil making that works due to the resistance of oil-based ink to water-based glue. Firstly, a positive image is painted, or drawn, onto a screen, using liquid tusche (a black oily ink), or lithographic crayon. When the ink design has fully dried on the screen, water-based glue is spread over the entire screen area. This is then left to dry. The positive image of tusche, or crayon, is then removed with white spirit. This leaves formerly inked-in parts of the screen as open spaces to be printed, for, although white spirit will soften and dissolve the tusche image, it leaves the water-based glue screen filler stencil unaffected.

This process can only be used for printing with oil-based inks: if water-based inks were used, the stencils would quickly break down.

Materials and preparation

Tusche
Liquid tusche is a black ink used mainly in lithography. In appearance it is not unlike a slightly oily indian ink. It can be obtained from either lithographic, or screen printing suppliers.

Before use, shake the bottle well. If the ink is too thick, add a small amount of water and stir thoroughly. Ink that is too thin can be adjusted by leaving to soak on newspaper. Pour a small amount of ink onto a folded paper. Once excess water has soaked into the paper, the ink can be tipped back into a container.

Lithographic and soft wax crayons
Lithographic crayons or any soft wax crayons can be used on their own, or in combination with a tusche design. They are

best used generously so that they fully fill the screen mesh.

Spirit duplicating carbon
Sheets of spirit duplicating carbon can be used to form a waxy drawn image. Simply lay a sheet, carbon side facing the supported screen, and draw over the back of the sheet with a pencil or ballpoint pen. The varying quality of line obtainable in this way can be used to add variety to the effects of tusche and wax crayon.

Stencil glue
The stencil glue should be strong, yet of a type that can be dissolved after setting. A permanent glue would ruin the screen. Le Pages Original Glue is both water-soluble after setting and resilient when dry. If you are unsure about a particular brand, test it before use. Spread some glue onto a small scrap of screen fabric, leave to dry and then see if it washes out easily.

Card
Small pieces of stiff card, such as mounting card off-cuts, are needed to apply the glue to the screen. They should be approximately 15cm (6in) long, with a straight cut edge. The straight edge will help ensure that the glue spreads evenly.

Method of working

1 If necessary, a drawing to work from can be taped to the baseboard and covered for protection with a sheet of

52 *Paint and draw in the areas to be printed using tusche and wax crayon*

53 *Scrape glue lightly over the whole format area*

acetate. Lower the screen down onto the baseboard. When using tusche, use lift-off adjustment or small pieces of card to ensure that the screen is about 3mm ($\frac{1}{8}$in) above the baseboard. This will prevent puddles of ink forming on the baseboard and creeping along the screen.

Start to paint and draw in the areas to be printed using tusche and wax crayon. In doing so, keep the painting bold, using ample ink to fill the mesh. Wax crayons should also be used strongly to penetrate the mesh fully. If ink or crayon merely coat the surface of the screen fabric, the process will not work as well. Mistakes can be blotted out with a wet cloth, or tissue, before the ink has dried.

2   Allow the tusche to dry. Remove the screen from the frame hinges. Support the frame about 2.5cm (1in) above the baseboard. This can best be done by placing two lengths of 5 × 2.5cm (2 × 1in) timber under opposite sides of the frame.

3   Pour glue, mixed to the consistency of thick cream, along one border of the screen. With a 15cm (6in) length of card, lightly scrape the glue over the entire format area, including the inked-in image. Use straight overlapping strokes to keep the coating even. When this is done, return any excess glue to the

54   *Wipe over entire image with a cloth soaked in white spirit*

container. Work the card scraper lightly across the screen in opposite directions to obtain an even finish. When dry, apply a second thin coat of glue using the same procedure. Try to keep both coatings of glue thin and as even as possible. At no time should the glue be allowed to seep through the screen and under the wax image.

4   Allow the glue to dry thoroughly. A fan heater can be used to speed up the drying time.

5   When thoroughly dry, place newspapers under the screen, and pour a liberal amount of white spirit over the inked-in image. Wipe over the entire image with a cloth soaked in white spirit (*Fig. 54*). Leave for at least one hour. This will allow time for the white spirit to soak into the ink and soften and loosen it. After this, rub over the image with a rag soaked in white spirit. Stubborn areas of ink can be gently scratched away with a finger nail, or old tooth-brush. General-purpose cleaner can also be used to help shift difficult areas.

6 Finally, clean the screen with fresh rags and leave to dry. Check for pin holes in the glued-in areas and spot these in with screen filler.

The stencil should now be ready for printing using oil-based inks. When finished with, the glue stencil can be removed with warm water. Tusche and glue stencils are quite robust, if made correctly, and should stand up well to printed use. The main points to bear in mind when making a stencil is a generous use of tusche and crayon when making the image, and thin coatings of glue when making the stencil, so as not to trap the tusche and wax crayon.

As a method of working, tusche resist has many advantages: with practice, the stencils are relatively quick and easy to make; the method is reliable; the qualities obtainable are interesting and different to those of other methods; unlike the sharp edges of a paper stencil, the printed results seem more in common with the broken lines, textures and soft edges associated with painting; because the image is painted straight onto the screen in a positive sense, there is also a certain directness in the method; incidental effects can sometimes occur through the process itself; stubborn areas of ink, that prove difficult to shift, can at times be left to form part of the stencil; Small areas that are left often add extra texture to a design, whilst larger areas may partly obscure an image to good effect, and a partially-explained image sometimes looks more interesting than one that has been overworked.

WAYS OF STORING PRINTS DURING DRYING

Wet ink can take from fifteen minutes to a few hours to dry thoroughly. During this time, wet prints need to be placed separately in such a way that air can circulate freely around them. They also need to be out of the way, to avoid becoming damaged or soiled.

Beginners should, for a while, be able to cope with placing the few prints made on chairs and table-tops around the room. But usually with experience comes the ambition to produce

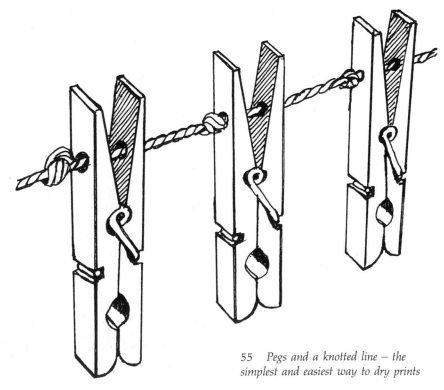

55 *Pegs and a knotted line — the simplest and easiest way to dry prints*

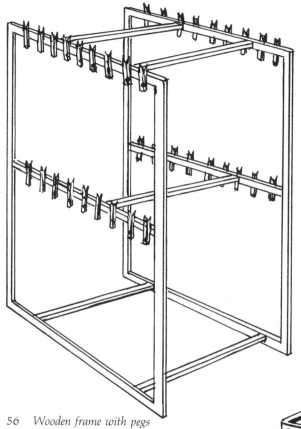

56   *Wooden frame with pegs*

pegs free movement of rotation.
Although this method is more rigid and secure than a line and less likely to damage prints, it is still very time-consuming.

Lightweight wooden racks
It is a simple task to construct lightweight wooden racks using thin battening. The shelves,

more and more prints at a time. Then, a simple system for efficiently drying prints safely will become necessary.

Pegs or paper clips and line
The simplest home-made way of drying prints is to use a line with pegs, or paper clips (*Fig. 55*). Holes should be drilled through the tops of the pegs. Both paper clips and pegs can be threaded onto a length of strong twine. Knots should be made at intervals between the pegs to stop them sliding together and spoiling prints.

Wooden frame and pegs
With reasonable space available, a more rigid system can be devised from a frame structure of thin battens and pegs (*Fig. 56*). The pegs should be secured to the battens with wire nails driven through the holes in the springs. Secure the nails just short of the spring, to allow the

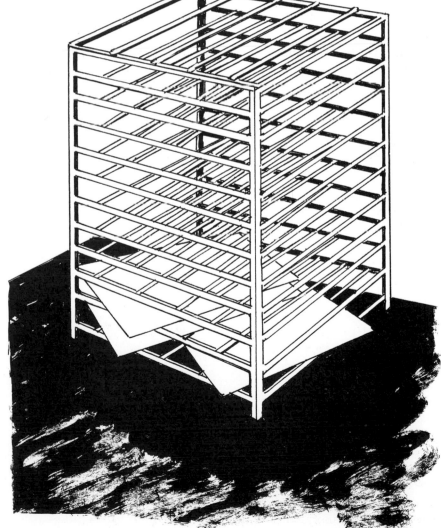

57   *Lightweight wooden rack*

which need to be about 5cm (2in) apart, can be supported by a number of thin plasterer's lathes (*Fig. 57*).

Stacking prints from the bottom upwards can be achieved in far less time than with pegs and line. With the corners of the prints overlapping the front of the rack, they can be collected up in a faster time when dry.

Spring-hinged metal drying racks

The best system for drying prints is undoubtedly spring-hinged metal drying racks (*Fig. 58*). They usually consist of a pile of fifty hinged trays, each of which is capable of holding two A1-sized prints. The open mesh construction ensures adequate support for prints, while still retaining good air circulation for drying. They are mounted on sturdy castors and can be easily moved.

Although the size and cost of metal drying racks can be prohibitive, they nevertheless provide the only really practical means of drying large editions. They are reliable and fast to use. Prints are stacked tray by tray, from the bottom up. If the prints are allowed to overlap the open front of the rack, they can be quickly removed in a reverse order.

The solution for storing prints during drying is to choose a method best suited to your particular needs. This will

58   *Spring-hinged metal drying rack*

depend on issues like the size of intended editions, print sizes, materials used, cost and available space.

Other popular methods of storage, apart from those mentioned, are stacks of

cardboard, or wooden, box-like trays, and ball racks.

PAPERS FOR PRINTING

The single largest consumable item in printing is paper. For economy, it is usually cheaper to purchase paper in bulk.

Wholesale paper agents usually sell paper by the 100 sheets. Sometimes, according to a particular manufacturer, it can be bought in mill packs of 50 sheets, or 125 sheets. Whatever the case, it is invariably cheaper than buying paper by the sheet.

When acquiring new printing stock, there are a number of considerations to bear in mind. Firstly, the cost needs to be balanced against the overall quality of a particular product. Secondly, features such as size, thickness and surface finish need taking into account, to ensure that the paper is suitable for what you have in mind. For instance, a paper with a pronounced textured finish would hardly be suitable for a design incorporating fine detail, whereas, for a broader image, relying on textural effects and atmosphere, it may be very fitting.

Experimenting on cheap paper

Apart from proofing and editioning, experiments with different methods, colour overprinting and new effects can provide a firm basis on which to develop ideas. At times like this, it is surprising how much paper gets used. In a single session it can pile up considerably, and the last thing one needs to worry about is the cost.

Fortunately, the versatility of screen printing is such that most types of paper can be used for experimenting on. Thin cartridge, sugar paper, newspaper and even wrapping papers can provide an inexpensive supply of material on which to try out new ideas.

General requirements for proofing and editioning

Although there are numerous types of paper available these days, only those that meet certain conditions will be serviceable as permanent printing stock. For proofing and editioning, only papers of good quality and permanence should be used. As a guide to choosing paper, some of these qualities are listed below.

Light proof

Cheap papers, like sugar paper, are not light proof and are unsuitable for permanent use. They will fade and yellow in time, especially when in contact with sunlight. If unsure about a particular paper, stick a sample piece against a window with a section masked out. After two weeks, remove the masked-out section and compare it with the rest of the paper.

Wood free

Wood free is a term applied to papers that have been made from chemically processed wood pulp. They are unlikely to fade or discolour, as cheaper ranges of papers processed by mechanical means often do.

Wood-free papers specially designed for printing, obtainable in weights of up to 300gsm, form a good middle range of papers for print-making. Heritage paper comes within this range.

For cheap proofing and editioning, a heavy cartridge is perhaps the most serviceable paper to use. A paper like Invernurie cartridge of 185gsm weight will provide a reasonable printing surface and thickness of material at low cost.

Strength and pliability

Papers need to be reasonably strong and pliable. Cheap paper, often produced from short-fibre pulp, cracks and creases easily.

Shrinkage

The way in which a particular paper is made and the raw materials used can add to or detract from its stability. Whereas all papers are susceptible to changes of atmosphere, the degree to which they do so can vary considerably. Papers that shrink and expand excessively with change are difficult to use and best avoided.

Cotton- and linen-based papers

The finest-quality printing papers are made from cotton or linen fibres. Traditionally they were made from cut rags, and even now they are often referred to as 'rag' paper, although synthetic fibre additives to cotton materials these days have made the use of rags impractical, and cotton linters are now used instead.

Apart from the stability and opacity of cotton as a raw material for paper making, it has long fibres which give added strength and flexibility to the paper. Flax is also used in making paper, the fibres of which are longer than those of cotton and result in very smooth-quality papers. There are a number of 100 per cent cotton papers available, in a variety of different sizes, weights and finishes.

Cotton- and wood-free mixtures. Added to the range of cotton- and wood-free papers are a number of products containing a percentage of cotton. The strength of wood-free paper is enhanced by a 20 to 40 per cent addition of cotton, whereas, the cost of a cotton paper is greatly reduced by the addition of 40 per cent wood fibre.

Hand-made and mould-made papers
As well as machine-made papers, there is a substantial range of hand-made papers available. These papers are of the highest quality, but sadly this is usually reflected in the high costs of such a labour-intensive process. Mould-made paper, however, is produced

using similar high-grade raw materials by a process similar to that of hand-made paper, but due to being mechanized the costs are far less. Both types of paper have deckle (rough) edges, which is characteristic of the general process.

Different paper finishes
Traditionally, paper is made to three main types of finish: *Hot-press* is smooth; *not* is slightly textured, and *rough*, as suggested, is textured. Although a manufacturer's description will give you some indication of what to expect, it often pays to send away for samples. This will also give you a better idea as to the exact degree of whiteness, tone or colour of a paper.

Changes of atmosphere and humidity

When proofing or editioning, it is advisable to keep to a constant atmosphere. Any violent changes of conditions, such as swings in temperature, could alter the paper shape, resulting in poor and inaccurate colour registration. For this reason, the printing stock should be left in the vicinity of the printing area for about a week prior to printing, to allow time for the paper to acclimatize to the atmosphere. Likewise, it is inadvisable, when printing, to use any form of direct heat to speed up drying times between colours. The use

of a fan heater, for instance, would dry out the moisture content of the paper, causing it to shrink considerably. The weight, or thickness, of the paper is no deterrent against this. A 300gsm paper will shrink as readily as one half the weight. The best way to facilitate drying times is to place the drying rack near an extractor fan. Movement of air over the prints will shorten the drying time, without any adverse effects.

DESIGNING YOUR OWN EMBOSSED PRINT SEAL

If you browse around galleries or shops selling original prints, you will probably notice that a number of designs have a small logo, or lettering, embossed on the bottom margin of the image. This is usually the artist's personal mark. Publishers, or print studios, occasionally add their seal to show that a particular edition of prints has been commissioned and published, or printed by them. Due to this, more than one mark may be present on a design.

Sometimes referred to as 'chop marks', these designs, made from a seal, both authenticate a work and provide a sense of personal identity. The seal, mounted in a small press, is simple to operate, taking only a short time to emboss each print.

Designing a personal seal

The design of a personal seal can be an interesting project in itself. An obvious solution is a monogram made up from your initials. The name of your studio, or house, can also be used, or, failing this, a simple logo. My own seal (*see Fig. 61*) was based on an elevated view of the printing process: the end of the blade, pressed over to the angle of printing, pushing down the line of the screen. '1838 Fine Arts' derived from a former trading name that I have used for a number of years.

In designing a mark, work to at least twice the size of the finished result. Even if the design is three or four times the intended size, it can be reduced down by the printer. In doing so, any small faults will seem to disappear. Although a seemingly easy task, to arrive at a suitable design can take a considerable time. A strong, simple silhouetted shape, with or without lettering, can make a striking design. Try to avoid anything too complicated, and keep the image simple.

Professionally-made seals

Once you have arrived at a suitable choice of design for the seal, the options are two-fold. You can produce the finished art work required for making up the seal. A positive cut in red masking film is the easiest way of achieving this. Cut the design two times larger than

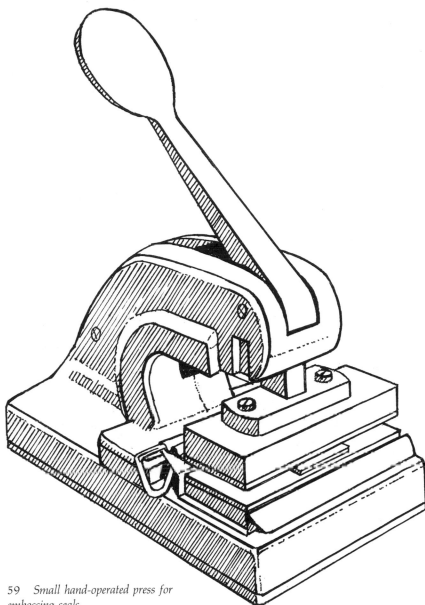

59   *Small hand-operated press for embossing seals*

the actual size. Alternatively, if you feel unsure of doing this, present the rough design to the printer. He should be able to get the finished art work produced at a small extra cost. If the design incorporates lettering, it is wiser to let the printer typeset it.

From the finished art work a pair of metal plates is then made up, consisting of one male and one female part. The plates are then set, in exact correspondence, onto a small hand-operated press, similar to that used for an address stamp

(*Fig. 59*). Easy to operate, these small presses sometimes have a variable marker guide which ensures that the embossed mark can be placed each time at the same height on the paper.

Simple home-made seals

If you like the idea of having a personal seal, but do not wish to incur the expense of having one made, it is possible to design and make up a simpler substitute. This can be made up as a small one-part metal plate and should work reasonably well for small editions. With a jewellery piercing saw, a shape or simple logo can be cut from a piece of sheet copper, or zinc. When glued and mounted on a small block of plywood, a home-made seal such as this can be pressed, or hammered against the border of a print and will make a reasonable impression (*Fig. 60*). Although the indentation will not be as deep or crisp as that made with a two-part seal, it will nevertheless serve as a personal identification mark in the same way as its more expensive counterpart.

Rubber stamps

A further alternative, and again far less expensive than an embossing seal, is to have a rubber stamp bearing a personal mark made up (*Fig. 61*). With this, you could print your mark on the border of the print using a light colour, in order not to confuse or detract from the image. This type of identification mark was used in France by gallery owners and publishers towards the turn of the century. Once again, any large printing firm should be able to help you get a stamp made up. To have this done the printer will require finished art work for the design or logo.

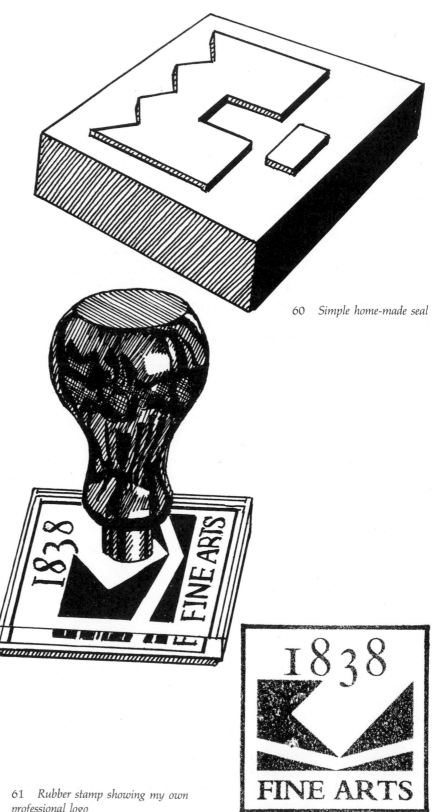

60   *Simple home-made seal*

61   *Rubber stamp showing my own professional logo*

3 DESIGN FOR PRINTING

An important aspect of screen printing is the initial planning and designing of imagery. The issues involved in a particular design or idea need to be well thought out before any stencils are made. One cannot so simply add a few dabs of extra colour to amend faults as one can with painting. Although changes can be made to prints part-way through the process, it is better not to have to do so, for even small failings take time and energy to remedy.

To start with, the choice of imagery used in designs for screen printing is worth careful contemplation. Certain subject areas are more easily adapted to the medium of screen printing than others. What will make an exciting screen print will not necessarily work well as a painting, and vice versa. For instance, interiors and furniture are favourite sources for screen printing images. A simple arrangement of plastic garden chairs, with sharp mechanical edges and patterned framework, could look very effective as a screen printed image. By using hand-cut stencils, this sort of imagery can also be achieved very easily.

In general, the choice of subject matter will depend partly upon the method of stencil-making that you intend to use. Any subject that can be best interpreted with crisp-edged shapes, or where straight edges and line are needed, will work well with hand-cut stencils. Images requiring broken, or softer effects, such as landscapes, will possibly work better using the tusche resist method of stencil-making. Other ideas might translate better by working directly onto the screen.

A good way in which to obtain experience is to visit galleries, or exhibitions, showing screen prints. By doing this and examining how particular prints have been made, it is possible to gain a broader knowledge as to how best to work out solutions when designing prints. When looking at prints, try to decide how many printings have been used, what type of stencils have been used and how any problems of registration have been overcome. Try to see yourself in the position of the artist who made the print. In this way you can pick up useful information and tips.

As you gain experience in designing and producing prints, no doubt you will begin to formulate a more personal way of working. For instance, in making prints, some people prefer to work, throughout all procedures, to a master tracing of the design, while others start with a design, only to revert to working from the actual print once one or two colours have been printed. There is no right or wrong way of developing a personal way of working. If the end results justify the means, then it will be worthwhile.

In starting screen printing, there is much to be said for keeping to a set of reasonably stringent guide lines. In this way you can gain experience without having too many failures. From that point on, it is very much a question of trial and error, developing your particular needs and interests in a personal way.

STRONG DESIGNS FROM DRAWING NEGATIVE SPACES

The stronger and more robust the drawing can be made, the more interesting will be the design and final printing. Designs, especially those made with very limited colours, need to be strongly executed, with a good framework of interesting shapes. One way of achieving this is to draw in a way known as the 'negative space' or 'left-over shape' method. To do this, one simply draws the spaces left between objects, rather than drawing the objects themselves, making it possible to create a better-proportioned and more original type of drawing.

Take, for example, the drawing of part of a castor oil plant (*Fig. 62*). Instead of drawing the leaves, the background (left-over shape) was first lightly plotted in. This consisted of numerous edges of different leaves; the shape plotted how each one was placed in general agreement to the arrangement overall. After defining the silhouette, the drawing was continued by building up the many shapes left between leaves and stems. Working in this manner, it was easy to produce a feeling of perspective in the leaf masses. By building up the structure and relating these smaller left-over spaces, the drawing was developed in an abstract way. A different sort of drawing emerged to that which would have been produced from drawing the leaf shapes themselves.

Drawing by using negative spaces can help us to look at and define more accurately the subjects we find of interest. With objects that we know, we are bound to have preconceived ideas as to how they should look. A leaf, tree, or boat is difficult to perceive clearly, without previous memories of such things clouding our memories and judgements. Yet the shapes between, or around, such objects are entirely new and different. They have no former meaning; we have no former recollections as to how they should look – they are meaningless. Because of this, it is possible to draw things in this manner with the spaces around them, in a fresh way with a judgement unclouded by previous memories.

In finding subjects to draw in this way, look for those that present an open network of varied and interesting negative shapes. By being selective, it is possible to simplify a drawing to a point where only a few simple hand-cut paper stencils need be used. Most subjects are able to be interpreted with three stencils in terms of tonality. The effect of using one light stencil, one half-tone and one dark stencil can usually be very satisfying. The simplicity of forming a jigsaw-like image in this way works very well in terms of the screen printing medium. It can also act as a firm basis for more elaborate designs.

Instead of using just three stencils, additional stencils to carry the effects of extra colour and textures can be introduced. In doing this, it is possible to add to an image without fear of confusion, because the basis of the image has first of all been clearly set out by the three tonal stencils that tend to hold the overall design in balance.

KEY IMAGE STENCIL AND SUPPORTING COLOURS

One possible difficulty of screen printing in various colours is to get the different parts of the design, printed with separate colour stencils, to relate and agree in an overall balanced way. Even with a colour sketch

for reference, it is sometimes difficult to visualize how six or seven stencils will overprint. At times, the results can look very uneven and unfinished. It can be difficult to judge the amount of work and detail required and the intensity of colour needed in making and printing a set of stencils for a particular image. One cannot simply add extra dabs of colour here and there, as in painting.

A simple and straightforward way around this problem is to make one of the stencils stand out far more than the rest. By starting with this one main stencil which incorporates most structure and drawing, and which will be printed with the darkest or strongest colour, a sense of unity is immediately created. Difficulties, such as alignment of stencils and registration during printing, are also minimized. Instead of being on a number of stencils, the drawing and strongest tones are carried on the one stencil. This main stencil can act rather like the pen work in a pen and wash drawing. It can provide a framework over which to print other stencils, so that you are adding extra colours, tones, patterns and textures to a print that already has a strong sense of unity and completeness. This method of working, with a 'key' image stencil and supporting colours, works particularly well for complex images. Any amount of fine detail can go

62   *Drawing of the negative spaces
around a caster oil plant*

into the key image stencil, without worrying as to how it will balance with other parts of the design, for one can see at a glance how the overall design will look from this one stencil image. The following stencils will add colour, tones and modifications which, although important, are more fine-tunings to the image than an intrinsic part of it.

The key image method can be applied to any of the stencil-making processes, from working directly onto the screen to hand-cut stencils, and from using tusche resist method to positive photo stencil methods. However, there is possibly more scope in producing the key image stencil through the use of positive stencil-making techniques. With either the tusche resist method, or the cut or drawn photo stencil method, there is not the need to think in terms of making negative stencils — it is done for you. What you cut out and draw in a positive way will print in a positive sense. This, in itself, affords more leeway to work in a less-constrained way and to be able to work with more detail. When working with a photo positive as the key image, there is almost limitless scope.

Using a photo stencil in this way, can be achieved without specialist equipment, by using the help of a commercial screen printer. It need not be prohibitively expensive. This, together with making a key image photo stencil, is more fully described in Chapter 5.

Working directly from a subject in a key image way

By using the tusche resist method to produce a key image drawing, it is practical to work directly from a subject. It is possible to take outside a bottle of tusche, a few brushes and a screen to draw on. In this way one can produce a vigorous landscape or townscape drawing, directly on the spot. As with painting, working directly from a subject on a screen can result in a more spontaneous and lively approach. Something of the impact and atmosphere felt about a particular scene, or subject, is often easier to portray firsthand, rather than working from drawings afterwards. Once the direct tusche drawing or painting has been made outside, it can be brought in and dried, ready for processing (see tusche resist method). Further stencils, using the same or different methods, can then be made.

Because the initial tusche resist image, made outside, will be complete in itself and print with the darkest and strongest colour, the additional stencils should be easy to make. They will need to align only roughly with the primary image, in this way adding extra colour and substance to the image, without detracting from the spontaneity. When working outside in this manner, it is worthwhile taking more than one screen with you. A drawn and painted tusche image need take no longer than working with ink on paper. By making more than one image at a time, it is usually possible to work more freely and not be so conscious of making mistakes. In addition, there is the advantage of being able to choose the better image.

COUNTERCHANGE OF TONES

A useful and often dramatic way of improving the appearance of an image is to use a counterchange of tone (*see p. 114*).

In this way, variety can be infused into a design, without the need for extra colours. In fact a strong image that makes good use of tone in a counterchange sense can look very effective printed in just one colour. Apart from looking more varied, an image that has counterchanged tones will often seem to knit together more effectively and appear fuller.

One of the easiest ways of experimenting with counterchange effects is with the use of hand-cut paper stencils. If both the cut-away parts of the stencil are saved, as well as the stencil itself, it is possible to print any part of the image light against dark, or dark against light: it will merely be a question of which part of the stencil you use to print with.

When using the small cut-away areas as a stencil, they will need to be held in place on the screen with a dab of glue that will not be soluble with the printing ink you use. (Water-based glue should be used if you intend using oil-based ink. When printing with water-based inks, use either lacquer or transparent base). If the design requires close registration, the small isolated pieces of stencil can be carefully positioned over a master tracing with the screen on top. Dabs of glue can then be painted over the mesh to hold these smaller pieces in place. When dry, the stencil can be printed.

Instead of printing a colour, the areas around these parts of the image, being open screen, will print instead, giving the design a counterchange effect. Depending on which parts of the stencil you print from, positive or negative parts, the printed outcome can look quite different in appearance. It is a worthwhile experiment to cut several facsimile stencils and print from them using different parts of the stencil.

Counterchange can just as simply be used with other methods of stencil-making, apart from cut paper stencils. The use of masking fluid and scratched effects on acetate positives, explained in Chapter 5, can be used to create a seemingly-unlimited variety of light imagery set against a darker printed background. Direct painting on the screen with glue, or lacquer, similarly produces a reversed-out image.

Used in combination with the tusche resist method, direct painting on the screen can create rich varieties of both reversed-out image against dark printed background and coloured image set against a light backing. When designing printed images, an important aspect is to realize the possibilities to hand, so that, after a little practice, printed designs and images will not always necessarily be dark against a lighter background. Variety of any kind is a useful device and should be fully used.

COLOUR: THE EFFECTS OF OVERPRINTING

Coloured prints are created from a series of overprintings of different colours; in other words, they are formed like a sandwich of colour. To get the best out of a medium like screen printing this has to be borne in mind. Each successive image has to add strength and interest in relation to the print as a whole. As a simile, think of a piece of plywood: with each thin layer of wood the grain runs in an opposite direction.

The sum total of these layers provides a stronger substance than the equivalent thickness in plain wood. Printed colour can work in the same way.

You will understand this more fully once you have created some overprinted designs of your own. Using an A4 format, try overprinting with primary colours – yellow, red and blue – utilizing simple torn paper stencils. With each colour, arrange the torn shapes in random fashion, overlapping but not copying the direction of shapes used for previous colours. If you print, for instance, five impressions of each image, you can gain added variation by occasionally turning the screen around and printing the image upside-down.

In the making of a series of prints such as this, using just three primary colours, the overprinting will achieve a range of secondary colours. Where just the blue and yellow overlap, a green will occur, and with red and yellow an orange, etc. In all, it is possible to achieve yellow, red and blue, plus green, orange, purple and brown: seven distinctive colours from the use of three.

You might think it easier to avoid such issues by not overprinting, by printing colours side by side, and so you can. Yet much of the fun and strength of print-making is in anticipating the subtle effects that can result from overprinting.

Printing colour chart strips

One useful way of predicting the results of overprinted colour is to produce a printed colour chart. Mix, for instance, six different colours. Using cut-paper stencils, print colours 1 and 2 in the form of a cross (*Fig. 63*). Then, using thinner rectangles, print colours 3 to 6 in turn, so that they intersect in the centre, like spokes in a wheel. The resulting colour chart can be stored for future reference.

Starting with light colours

It is best to work from light to dark, from muted to intense colour. The first one or two colours can extend over large parts of, or the whole, print area, acting as a background, leaving, if necessary, an occasional area of paper to show through. Successive stencils — the half tones — can be more elaborate and will possibly cover smaller surfaces. The final darks or intense colours can be used to balance the design and add detail.

Designs using watercolour

The above description of how colours in a print are usually built up could easily double as a definition of watercolour technique, though there are, of course, differences. Screen printing produces all-over areas

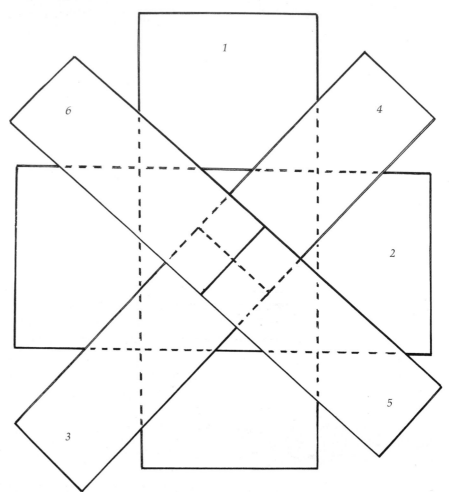

63   *Overprinting six different colours in a colour chart*

of flat colour, and cut-out stencils simplify the imagery. Yet, in the main, the processes are not dissimilar.

As a result of this, ideas and themes can be pre-tested using colour studies, and time and effort saved by avoiding unlikely ideas. As these studies will, at best, act only as a guide, it is easier to carry them out on a small scale. After drawing the initial design in pencil, thoroughly mix quantities of each colour you are likely to use in separate dishes, or saucers. After you have used a colour, wash the brush thoroughly and wait for the colour to dry before applying the next one. Taking these precautions will help

ensure that the colour is of a more even nature and compatibility to printed colour.

Coloured inks

Coloured inks can be used with, or in a similar way to, watercolours. Because they stain, rather than settle on the surface like watercolour, underlying colours are less likely to shift, or mix with succeeding colours. This can result in sharper imagery and clearer overlapping colour shades, providing a nearer comparison to print quality.

Coloured felt-tipped pens and layout paper

Coloured felt-tipped pens work very effectively on layout paper, which is produced in pads. This is a popular method used by professional designers and graphic artists for visualizing printed colour. Used on thicker, or softer-textured, paper, the pens quickly run out or go blotchy, due to the fact that they are spirit-based. On layout paper, however, they produce well-defined edges and do not blur or mix with underlying colours. The semi-transparent nature of this type of paper is also useful, in that different colour images can be made over the original one without having to redraw each one.

Any felt-tipped pens will work, and there is a wide variety on the market, from cheap sets for children, to the more expensive and subtle products used by designers.

Coloured pencils

For quickness and ease of use, coloured pencils are unbeatable. Used in combination with layout paper, as above, one can try out numerous ideas, on a small scale, in a very short time. They are also invaluable for indicating colour on full-scale pencil or pen drawings. Colour hints can be added without losing the crispness and definition of line, as would be the case with, for instance, watercolour. Apart from ordinary coloured pencils, there are wide ranges of watercolour pencils available. These can be bought in boxed sets of up to forty colours, and last a long time.

64   *Rubbings can give some idea of overprinted stencils*

SILHOUETTED FIGURES AS A SOURCE OF DESIGN

People seen in everyday life can provide a constant source of print design. In a never-ending range of changing postures and clothing, seen singly or as groups, they make an ideal theme. With active pursuits like running, dancing, swimming and gymnastics, etc., the diversity of shape and line are magnified, and a new ingredient – movement – is added. They work well in screen printing as simple cut-out shapes, enhanced by areas of flat or blended colour with sharp edges.

Even if you cannot draw, this idea can still work well. Fashion magazines are full of photographs of people in varying attitudes, many of them displaying a sense of movement. After selecting a few that look promising, carefully cut them out, using a sharp craft knife, or a scalpel. In screen printing, they can be used as direct stencils: simply arrange them on the printing paper, then place the screen on top. After the first pull of ink, they will stick to the screen in the usual way. Try using straight-edged shapes to go with them; the shapes of rectangles etc. should contrast nicely with the flowing lines of the figures. As an extension of this idea, overprint using different figures and colours each time. Apart from heightening the sense of movement, this can lead to exciting effects of overprinted colour and incidental shapes, which can add intrigue and mystery to the finished design.

To gain a rough idea of how a build-up of figures and shapes, in different overprinted colours, will look, rubbings made with coloured wax crayons can be useful. For this, trace the magazine figures onto thick paper, like sugar paper, and cut them out; do likewise with other shapes. Arrange these on a smooth surface and place a sheet of thin paper, either newspaper or, better still, layout paper, over the top and secure the corners with drawing pins or tape. Rub evenly over the surface using the side of a coloured wax crayon.

Once completed, rearrange the figures, or use new ones and continue the process using a different coloured crayon. After two or three colours, they should gain interest with the effects of overlapping colour. As this method is both simple and fast, once the figures are cut out it should be easy to produce numerous variations of design and colour combinations in a short period of time.

65 *Initial idea in collage for* Water Meadow

COLLAGE

A simple collage, made from torn or cut pieces of coloured paper, is possibly the nearest one can get to the natural outcome of simple screen printed images. The results are not at all unlike those printed from paper stencils. This is due to several reasons. Firstly, the

66 Daisies *by Maria Mathers*

67   Dancers *by Dorothy Williamson.*
Printed from paper stencils using figures
cut from pages of fashion magazines

68   Tree *by Maria Mathers. Incorporating the use of ready-made stencils*

general characteristics of cut or torn shapes are very different from drawn or painted images. Cut-out images have a crispness and vigour which would be difficult to imitate in a drawn or painted sense. Secondly, the simplicity and compactness with which either collages or simple screen prints can be put together is not dissimilar. Added to this is the natural appearance of simple screen printed colour – flat even colours with sharp edges – which is not unlike that produced in collage. In general, the two mediums can be very similar in appearance.

For these reasons collage as a medium is very appropriate for working out and visualizing simple screen printing ideas and images. When working with collage, in place of cut or torn paper stencils, one can see at a glance whether or not a particular avenue of thought is worth pursuing. For, in essence, the finished results of the design and printed results will be much the same. It helps to solve the problem of having to visualize how a design produced in one medium will look when translated to a printed state with different characteristics.

In addition to this, collage is an exciting medium in its own right, fun to do and easy to carry out. One obvious advantage is the flexibility with which designs can be made. A collection of torn or cut shapes can be moved around indefinitely on a piece of paper, the format of the intended design. Instead of being left wondering how a design could have looked with this or that changed or moved around, one can find out immediately.

As the various elements of the design become established, they can be fixed with a dab of glue to hold them in place. Once the overall design is finalized, the various parts can be carefully lifted and placed to one side. A thin layer of glue can be spread over the backs of the shapes with a spatula and the parts can then be glued down permanently. To save gluing, there are ranges of gummed-backed coloured papers. These are very convenient to use, but since they are mainly designed for use in schools, the range of colours is usually very limited.

To have a wider option of colours, it is better to paint washes of colour on sheets of paper beforehand. By experimenting with various groupings of small patches of colour, painted side by side, a range of colours suitable for the design and print can be decided upon. In this way, it is possible to produce workable colour schemes.

When starting on a collage, it is easier to cut out and place large background shapes first, and then to build the image over these with smaller arrangements of cut or torn shapes of different colours. This will avoid small gaps of background paper showing through. It will also give the design more sense of breadth and unity. Interestingly, the same can be said for designing and making the stencils with which to print from.

Overprinting and coloured tissue paper.

One problem, when designing prints, is knowing how the effects of overprinted colours will look. If, for instance, a green is to print over a purple, what would the resulting colour be? Even if it is possible to guess the right result of any two overprinted colours, it is impossible when three or four colours are involved.

The use of coloured tissue paper can provide as good an answer as any to such concerns. It is transparent to the extent that overlayed colours show up clearly, and unlike other mediums, such as transparent inks, paints, or coloured pencils, the results of overlaying various colours can be prejudged before they are finalized. Different colour combinations of tissue paper can be laid out, changed and changed again, before they are glued in place. In a very short time you will find that it is possible to gain valuable experience as to the results of

69   Collage using flat colours and cut-out areas of striped pattern from magazines

overlaying numerous combinations of colour.

When a scheme is finalized, careful handling and the correct glue need to be used for sticking down the various layers of coloured paper. If this is not done, the various colours will dissolve in the glue and mix together, muddling up the outcome. To expand the range of colours available, white tissue paper can be painted, before use, with washes of coloured ink, dye or watercolour.

The results of collages made in this way should approximate more readily than other mediums to the possible effects of overprinted colour.

Collages from printed material

There is a wealth of imagery that can be gleaned from printed sources. With the ever-increasing numbers of newspapers, colour supplements and magazines available, it is not difficult to find plenty of material that could be useful for making collages. Different bits and pieces of torn or cut imagery can simply be assembled and pasted down to form a basis for new ideas. Master tracings can then be made from the collage effects, from which stencils can be made in the usual way. By the time the designs have been printed, they will most probably have gone through a process of simplification, the results of which often have more impact and vigour than

the original collages.

At the other end of the scale is a fashion, popular amongst some contemporary artists, for using collages from printed matter in their entirety. The process enabling one to do this is very expensive and technical. The various colours in the design are separated, by photographic means and using different colour filters, into various half-tone colour positives. Photo stencils are then made up and the collage is printed, often to facsimile likeness. Hand-cut photo positives are often used in such works, to obtain greater unity and depth of colour. But for practical reasons and those of cost, this way of working is out of most people's reach.

Working in a simplified way from collages can produce very

imaginative results. The kind of imagery arrived at by these means can look quite different in character to anything achieved by purely drawn or painted methods. The seemingly never-ending supply of imagery just needing to be selected from and rearranged can act as a springboard for developing fresh ideas and images. It is the one medium where it is almost impossible to run out of new ideas.

Being quick and easy to make, a whole series of small collage designs can be built up in a day. Often parts of these assembled designs can look more interesting than the design in total. Different sized and proportioned viewfinders can be cut from paper, or offcuts of mounting card. By moving these over larger collages, new and often more-exciting images can be discovered. Just a slight change in the juxtaposition and proportions of a group of coloured shapes can at times spark off new ideas. Even dull-looking collages can sometimes be brought back to life with this sort of treatment. An alternative way of working is to cut two L-shaped mounts; the two parts can be brought together to form an adjustable rectangular mount. By using this, you can quickly decide on the possibilities of changing the format size.

Selecting from images

already in existence and re-forming them can be less arduous, more fun, and make a change from always working in a drawn and painted sense. Formulating designs from cut up bits and pieces of photographs from magazines, and then selecting from parts of the collage design, is an auto-suggestive way of working. It can in itself act as a catalyst for totally new ideas that have little in common with the actual images you might happen to be working with at the time. A combination of shapes here or a colour there may suggest a lead to something very different, and thus the process acts as a stimulus to the imagination. In the same way, just collecting together interesting photographs and pages from magazines etc. can provide a reservoir of ideas for future use. Glancing through them, when visually at a low ebb, can lead to new directions and ideas.

USING PHOTOCOPIERS FOR DESIGN

Photocopiers can provide a useful adjunct to design. Readily available, these often highly-sophisticated machines are now a common sight in libraries and shops, and every office, college and school seems to own one. For a few pence a copy, they are cheap to use. The other main advantages are that they work instantaneously and are simple to use. By

resetting the contrast control, a strongly-contrasting black and white copy can always be made.

Reducing images to black and white can have interesting results. Areas of tone seem to collect together in a sense that can look very atmospheric and imaginative. The process seemingly transposes grey and shadowy areas with peculiarly distinctive mottled half tones. Parts of photographs and printed designs etc., cut or torn from magazines, can be pasted down on a background to re-form new images. Then, with process white and black ink, or water-based black paint, the design can be worked into and further adapted. The result can then be photocopied and, if necessary, further changes made and photocopied again. The whole process can be completed in a short time.

Designs made in this way can either be used directly, or indirectly. To use them directly will require the services of a commercial printer. For a small cost, he will be able to make, from a good contrasting photocopy provided by you, a photo positive on clear acetate. From this a photo stencil can then be made. Worked from indirectly, you can use the photocopy as a master copy from which to make cut-paper, or film stencils, etc. Apart from its appeal as an immediate way of working, this method of

70   Leaves *by Maria Mathers*

71   Dancers *by Maria Mathers*

building up images is ideal for anybody with unsure drawing ability.

Apart from straightforward photocopying, most copiers these days have a facility to either reduce or enlarge material. This greatly enhances their usefulness. Parts of designs can be enlarged to three or four times their former size, often with surprising results. Apart from printed material, small sections of black and white pen drawings etc. can be enlarged, the effects of which can often look more vigorous and exciting than the original. When printed photographs or drawings are repeatedly enlarged, the imagery and tones gradually tend to break down. This in itself can produce an interesting range of textures and broken effects.

Certain photocopiers are able to copy onto materials other than paper; some will copy onto special sheets of clear acetate film. Provided that the quality is good, this is a far more direct and less-costly way of producing a photo positive. It can be made immediately, rather than waiting to have the photocopy photographed onto acetate.

Quite apart from printed matter and drawings, all sorts of materials can be used for making worthwhile photocopies. Anything that is flat enough, has an interesting silhouette or openwork pattern or texture can be used. Keys, plastic drawing instruments with measurements on them, skeletal plant forms, small metal grids and all manner of things can look interesting when photocopied. The results can be used on their own, or cut out and pasted down, forming mixed designs using parts of photographs, to make more complex images. Textures and patterns photocopied from bits and pieces of open-weave fabrics are useful. Often the materials themselves are too thick to be printed directly as found stencils.

Solarized effects of using photocopiers

An unusual side effect, which arises from using different thicknesses of material to copy from, is that a counterchange of tones can be simply achieved. This seems to be dependent on whether or not the copying material is pressed tightly against the glass and lid of the copier, and on the thickness of the material. Where there is good contact between the glass and lid, the material used will print as a strong black positive image. Where there is space between the material used and the glass and the lid, the result is likely to be a solarized effect – the tones are reversed. In other words, parts of the material not pressed tightly against the glass will appear white against a dark background.

The photocopy of the weathered remains of Chinese lanterns is a good example of this (*Fig. 72*). Towards the edges of the image the lantern shapes appear black against a white background; towards the centre of the image where the plants overlap and build up a thickness, the lanterns and stems print light against a black background. Although this occurred unintentionally, the effect achieved was more interesting than if the whole image had been dark against a light background.

It is quite possible, by trial and error, to make the effect of solarization work in an intentional and design sense. By deliberately arranging various thicknesses of material under a copier, it is possible to predict, to some extent, the counterchanged outcome.

DESIGNS AND STENCILS MADE FROM RUBBINGS

Patterns and textures of all kinds can work well in a printed sense. They can add variety and a new sense of dimension to an image, especially one printed in limited colours. Yet, painted by hand, intricate patterns can be difficult, time-consuming, and often very laborious to produce. This is where rubbings, made with wax crayons etc., can provide a quick and easy answer. Any interesting

72 *Photocopy of Chinese lanterns,*
showing solarized effect

material, or surface, that is hard enough so that a rubbed impression can be made is worth considering. When printing with water-based inks, these impressions can be made directly onto a screen and then used as a direct stencil. Candles and light-coloured wax crayons work well, applied directly to the mesh. When making the rubbings, it is important that neither the material from which the impression is taken nor the screen moves while the rubbing is being made. The slightest movement of either would produce blurred results. Also ensure that you build up a reasonably dense deposit of wax. Lightly-rubbed impressions will possibly not print.

Apart from working directly onto the screen, rubbings can be used as photo positives, for making photo stencils. Used in this way, it is the density of black pigment, rather than the thickness of wax impression, that counts. The paper used needs to be semi-transparent. Use black lithographic crayons and white tissue paper, or layout paper, to make the impression. As with direct rubbings, the impressions made need to be well defined. If the material from which the rubbing is to be made is not rigid, stretch it out on a drawing board using drawing pins or a staple gun. Over this, carefully tape down the paper before you start.

Once done, Chapter 5 on the photographic stencil process fully explains how you can process paper photo positives. The only difference is that these paper positives should not be soaked in white spirit or paraffin to make the paper more transparent; doing this would merely dissolve the lithographic crayon image. Instead, the rubbings should be exposed dry, possibly for a little longer to make up for the extra opacity of the paper. Making a test strip, prior to use, could help decide the correct exposure time needed. Wherever possible, use white tissue paper which, being that much thinner than layout paper, should not present any difficulties.

Rubbings can be made from a wide range of different materials. Those taken from wooden surfaces can look particularly attractive, with easily-found patterns from straight grains to swirling lines. Making use of such textures need not be complicated as they can be used in the simplest of ways. For instance, a well-defined and interesting large area of textured wood grain might well be used for the surrounding background of a still life. The resulting contrast between the realistic and decorative texture of such a background, set against the simple shapes of a few objects, could look very effective.

Fabrics can likewise provide a rich variety of usable pattern and texture. From openwork netting and lace, to coarsely-woven materials such as canvas,

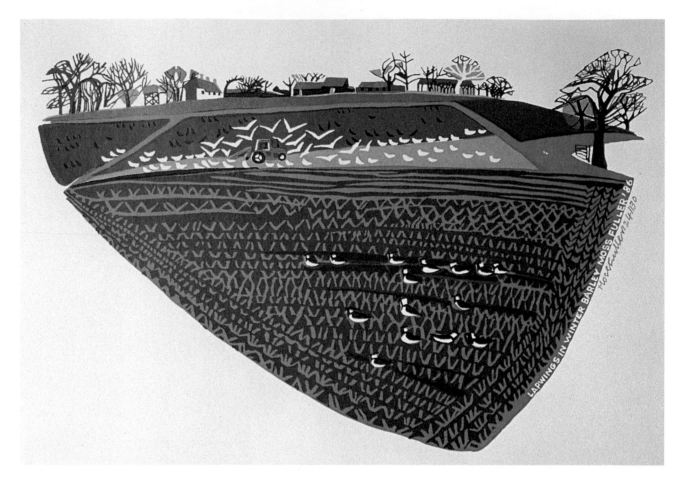

73 Landscape *by Moss Fuller showing a different-shaped print format*

differing textures and patterns can be gained. These, together with numerous other sources such as embossed wallpapers, metal grids and embossed plastics, can provide a wealth of added pattern and texture that can enrich and add contrast to all sorts of designs.

Apart from providing stencils, rubbings can be used just as a means of developing new ideas and finding out more about overprinted colour. Using layout paper, different rubbings can be built up over each other, with various coloured wax crayons, to give an indication as to the effect of several overlaid colours. It is a quick and simple process, building up a number of different overlaid colours. Plain areas can be achieved by rubbing over cut-

out areas of thick paper or thin card. The results from these experiments, taking up little room, can easily be stored in a drawer or folder until such times as they can be put to good use.

DIFFERENT-SHAPED PRINT FORMATS

At times the actual shape of the material from which a rubbing has been made might appear unusual and of interest by itself. It might, for instance, suggest the format shape for a print, quite different from the usual square or rectangular shape. Apart from the ease of registration, there is no practical reason why a print format should conform to any particular shape. A print can be any shape or size that you see fit to make it. There are not the same restrictions as with

alternative printing processess: you do not have to keep to within a printing plate size, serviceable by a printing press, as in etching or lithography. You have only to depend on the screen size that you see fit to make up in the first instance.

So, if you are inventively-inclined, one approach to design could be to choose an unusual-shaped format from which to start. By starting with a format, suggested from a piece of wood, metal, or a geometric shape such as a hexagon, the overall outcome of design is likely to be quite different. On the other hand, an idea or image could just as readily lead to a particular-shaped design. For instance, a gold fishpond might work well set in an oval or circular format, in a sense echoing the ideas in a rather novel way.

74   Canal Basin *by Maria Mathers*

75   Salt Marshes *by Maria Mathers*

On a slightly less-adventurous level, one might opt for a rectangle that does not necessarily have clean-cut straight-edged borders. Certain subjects might gain if the imagery is allowed to sprawl over the edges: landscapes, in particular, might gain in spontaneity if the edges are not kept in such perfect check. As with design in general, the outcome will largely depend on whether or not the components balance up and look right. There is a world of difference between a print with scruffy edges and one that has been designed in a spontaneous way with overlapping shapes.

LINE DRAWING IN PEN AND INK, AND PENCIL

Certain ideas will work better than others in screen printed form. In the same way, certain styles of drawing will be more successful than others. Before even attempting to make drawings with print-making in mind, consider for a moment what it is you are attempting to achieve. Try to think more in terms of the information you require for the idea and less about producing a drawing that will necessarily work in its own right. It is objective and informative statements that are usually required.

For instance, an indistinct and sketchy drawing supported by imaginative smudges of tone here and there might look effective and charming in its own right, but if you were to try to interpret such a work as a screen print, you would surely be disappointed. For while screen printing, as a medium, can be stretched in all directions, it still possesses certain inherent characteristics. The natural results of screen printing tend towards clarity, precision and evenness of printed tone and colour. Even broken lines and textures, printed from a single stencil, will result in an even flatness of colour. It is worth bearing in mind the qualities required and resisting the temptation to fumble over difficult areas with uncertain line and vague clouds of tone. So, when drawings are interpreted, first as a master tracing and then as a series of stencils, problems such as where to put a line will not arise.

Working in a clear-cut way does not necessarily mean that one's drawing will become rigid or stilted: quite the contrary; drawings made in this way often have more sense of directness and vigour, easily superseding various rambling efforts when clarity is not a prerequisite.

Pen and ink, in particular, is a good medium for drawing and making preliminary studies for screen printing. The medium itself prevents anything but a clearly-defined image being made. When using a pen and dense black ink, an added advantage is that the drawing will not rely at all on subtle variations of tone, thus making its interpretation into stencil form that much easier.

The choice of pens is very much a personal matter. There are excellent products widely available and cheaply priced. Amongst the cheapest are fibre-tipped pens, which can be obtained with a wide range of different thickness points. The finest ones are ideal for sketch book studies and depicting areas of detail and pattern. Black biros are useful – they are handy to carry around at all times, being less likely to leak – for jotting down small studies on scraps of paper. Rotring pens, whilst good to draw with, have a tendency to block up at inopportune moments. For this reason it is important to keep the tops on them, and for this same reason they are not so suitable for out-of-doors use. Likewise, dip-in pens are good for drawing indoors, but for outside work they are probably more trouble than they are worth. Apart from having to constantly redip the pen to replenish the ink supply, one has either to hold the bottle, or face the danger of it being knocked over.

When making studies for new ideas, one can never have too much information. Drawings can quite easily be simplified down: the basic elements can be used and certain detail can be eliminated from the final design. Seldom, however, is the reverse true: a drawing that might have seemed satisfactory at the point of making it can easily fall short of information later on, when you start to work from it.

It is wise to pursue just one idea, instead of making drawings of a wider variety of subject ideas. In this way, you will produce a series of studies giving ample information from which a print can be developed at a later stage. When out drawing and you discover a good subject, after making a study of it, stop to consider whether or not you have enough workable information, before moving on to try something different. It is far better to have sufficient drawings to make one good print, rather than have half a dozen that you may only find to be inadequate afterwards.

Pencils are easy to carry around and use in any situation. They do, however, need to be kept well-sharpened, otherwise the definition of drawing can suffer. A well-sharpened grade B for setting out the structure, and a 6B for putting in tones, will suffice for most situations. Thicker-leaded plain drawing pencils, sharpened to a chisel point, can be useful for blocking in areas of tone, especially when an image has a strong pattern of tonality. It is more effective to use the pencil

almost on its side, instead of on the point. By doing so, you will have a greater control over the depth of tone, and tones can be laid in quicker. A combination of pencil and fibre-tipped pen works very well when the subject has a strong sense of tonality, and structural drawing is needed.

DESIGNING WITH REGISTRATION IN MIND

When printing with more than one colour, registration plays an important role. From the offset of working out an idea, one should have in mind the means by which the design will eventually register. How you best achieve this will depend largely upon the kind of idea you have. But whatever that might happen to be, it is essential to think beforehand of how the print will register.

As far as possible, it pays to keep the amount of finite registration to a minimum. Wherever possible, use lighter colours broadly, so that a darker or brighter stencil will overprint and define the shapes. Try to avoid areas where shapes on two different stencils meet each other exactly around the edges. In circumstances where this cannot be avoided, make the lighter stencil slightly larger, with an overlap of 2mm ($\frac{1}{16}$in) around the edges. This will avoid slight areas of white

showing through in places where the printed stencils fail to meet properly. It is almost impossible, and usually not worth while, to cut or paint two shapes that correspond perfectly around their edges.

Another answer to this is to make a linear stencil that forms a line between the borders of the different colour areas. Often the same line work is used in areas to create patterns and detailed drawing. It is effective for certain subjects, but this way of working can look mechanical and rather monotonous. In the same way, lines are often printed around the borders of images to straighten up the somewhat irksome effects of poor and ragged registration.

Images designed with random registration
Designing an image where the shapes of one stencil necessarily have to correspond with the shapes of further ones is not always a virtue. It is the final printed result that always counts. Registration is, at best, only a means to an end. If the design is sparse or ill-conceived, no manner of carefully-aligned and well-registered stencils will save it. On the other hand, it is possible, with careful planning, to produce a successful image that relies very little on a close registration of shapes, other than alignment round the edges of the print.

76   *Two positives and corresponding printings for* July Meadow

July Meadow was just such a print. Out of nine stencils used for the printing, only two had closely corresponding sets of shapes (*Fig. 76*). These were the stencil that printed bright yellow, mainly for the flowers, and the stencil that cut around the shapes of the yellow flowers to print a darker background colour. The other seven stencils were designed and painted in a random way. Because of this, it was only thinking out how the image would work that was time-consuming. The actual stencil-making took a fraction of the time that making stencils relying on corresponding shapes would have taken, and the printing was uncomplicated. After proofing, with a few changes and some strengthening of image here and there, the design worked out very well. The editioned printing gained a strength and freedom not too dissimilar to a loosely-printed watercolour. The time saved in preparing the stencils alone made the venture worth while.

Obviously one cannot treat every kind of subject matter in the same free and easy manner. *Cats and Wisteria*, for instance, required a totally different approach. The very existence of the window, with its rigid architectural detail picked out in various tones, required a disciplined approach to alignment and registration of the numerous stencils used. However, making the set of stencils took about a year, on and off. In places the same shapes had to be cut or drawn around a dozen times in a most precise manner. Fortunately, the outcome was very successful. Yet it will be a long time, if ever, before I tackle such a difficult task again.

The best answer, as far as registration is concerned, is to take your time before finalizing the design. Think about the various ways of planning the image in mind, and weigh up the difficulties confronting you by taking this solution or that. As far as possible, try not to get bogged down in a lengthy struggle, trying to make a set of stencils that relies too heavily on a lot of tedious, closely-defined alignment of imagery. Wherever possible, look for an alternative route. Try to think in purely print-making terms and not those of picture-making or painting.

It is usually the case that creating a particular effect has to be weighed against the time and effort required to make the preparations, such as a set of printable stencils. You will probably find, in most cases, that a few extra hours spent thinking over alternative

77   *Greetings cards by Maria Mathers*

strategies can save you hours of tedious work spent in arriving at a solution to a design problem that might just as easily have been avoided. No matter how long it takes to make a set of stencils, and no matter how difficult the printing might be, it is the end result that finally counts, whether it has taken you a matter of hours or months.

If you feel unsure after reading this of how to go about planning with registration in mind, as good a way as any is to start with an all-over light printed colour. This will ensure that you are not left with any minute shapes of unprinted paper. You will be able to set about the task of stencil-making in a more relaxed manner, with the knowledge that parts that do not quite meet up as they should will go largely unnoticed. The first all-over flat, or blended, colour will give a sense of finish and unity to all that follows it. At the same time, you can use the first colour to set a mood or atmosphere to the particular design in mind. Even a relatively quiet colour, being printed over such a large area, will have a considerable effect, depending on whether it is, for instance, a cool blue or a warm yellow.

VARIATIONS OF DESIGN USING SIMPLE BASIC SHAPES

Screen printing is an ideal medium with which to develop and experiment with printed variations of simple imagery. By using cut-paper stencils and basic shapes to start with, it is possible to build up quickly any number of printed variations. The simplest of shapes can be used in this way. By printing the image in a variety of different grid patterns, the effects can appear quite different. A square, for instance, continually overprinted corner upwards, will immediately lose its sense of former identity. The same shape, overprinted a number of times, radiating from the centre outwards, can appear in a star-like formation.

Working in this manner has a particular significance if you happen to be interested in printing on fabrics. For even though these patterns do not necessarily have to repeat themselves in a rigid sense, they nevertheless can result in bold all-over patterns, the results of which can have many practical uses. Even if you keep this sort of printing to paper alone, it can be fun to do, and the results can be unexpected and exciting. What is more, you can learn a good deal as to how images can be built up and what the effects of numerous overprintings are likely to be.

A good point about this way of working is that you can be printing almost immediately, without any former planning. All you need to do is cut, for instance, a small L shape from a sheet of newsprint. Then start to print from this simple stencil, using a few mixed-up, or left-over colours. If working on paper, use water-based inks: you will find them far more practical and convenient to work with.

Initially, it is best just to overprint the L shape a number of times in a random fashion. From this, you should get some idea of the possibilities of printing it in a number of variations. It might be that two or three of the L shapes have overprinted in a particularly interesting way. This could simply be expanded by repeat printing this particular image over a sheet of paper. In doing so, you would probably find it more convenient to recut a paper stencil to the dimension of the three overprinted L shapes.

Conversely, it could be that the particular way in which the L shapes were printed as a whole was of interest. To expand this, they could be printed on a larger scale.

Considering the variety of basic shapes, the alternate manner in which they can be overprinted, and the various grid patterns and structures, it is easy to realize the endless possibilities of design that can be achieved. It is a method of working which is fun to do and where the results greatly outweigh the effort required to produce them.

POSTERS AND DESIGNS WITH LETTERING

Screen printing is the most efficient medium for producing posters, especially for designs larger than A4 size, or where limited numbers are required. It is flexible in terms of size, only requiring a screen to be made up that much larger than the design itself. Designing and making stencils to print from is simple, and takes little time when photo stencils are used. The printing itself, in one or two colours and up to a few hundred copies, is quick and easy to do. The thickness of ink deposited on the paper, being thicker than in other printing processes like offset lithography, improves the clarity and design impact.

Using photo positives
For the best results, it is advisable to use the photo stencil process. By doing this, one has merely to produce a sketched-out rough indicating the size and positioning of any lettering used in relation to the design. From this, any moderate-sized printing firm will be able to typeset the lettering and to transfer it onto litho film. It will probably be returned as separate lines of type, and you will have to

78 *Poster with lettering using varied techniques*

assemble these onto a sheet of clear acetate, securing them at the corners with small pieces of clear adhesive tape. This is best done using a light box, so that you can be assured that everything is in correct alignment. From then on, one has simply to process the photo positive in the usual manner.

The poster in Fig. 71 was made using varied techniques. Ordinary typeset lettering was produced in the way

described above. The slogan, at the top, was hand-painted on acetate using a brush and photo opaque – a quick-drying blocking-out medium. But the central design itself was made in a somewhat unusual fashion.

Firstly, a random list of courses was typed, using varied type-faces, as a solid pattern on a sheet of A4 paper. This was enlarged up a few times on a photocopier. A simple silhouette of figures was drawn and cut out of two of the photocopied sheets. This design was then dry-mounted onto thick cartridge paper, the background of which was painted in black ink. This was then simply photographically reproduced as a reversed-out image on litho film by the commercial printer, so that the photo positive, in this case really a photo negative, printed in tonal reverse of the typed and cut-out original. Finally, the poster was printed in blended colours, with blue at the bottom and orange at the top.

The design of geese for another poster was one of nine positives used for a limited edition print. This poster was also printed using blended colours. Printing blends of different colours is a useful device insofar as posters are concerned. It allows the work to be carried out in a single printing, with a variety of colours.

As an alternative to having type set for you, it is quite possible to use any of the transfer type sheets that are readily available in art shops and stationers. They are usually stocked in reasonable varieties of different type-faces. Unless you require very large lettering, you should be able to find something adequate. They are also easy to use. All you have to do is to place each letter, one at a time, over the design (in this case on clear acetate) and rub over the back with a pencil to release the letter. A

79   Figure *by Nicholas Bristow. Oil pastel print*

straight line drawn on paper and placed under the acetate should help you to line the lettering up. Using transfer lettering for photo positives is particularly practical when only a small amount of lettering is required. For items such as greeting cards, where one or two words will suffice, it is by

far the better way.

Printing lettering without the use of photo stencils is possibly best achieved by using one of the hand-cut film stencil methods. However, this can be a lengthy and tedious procedure, and small-sized lettering is all but impossible to do. The other alternative is to trace the lettering onto the screen with a sharp pencil, and to paint around it using a

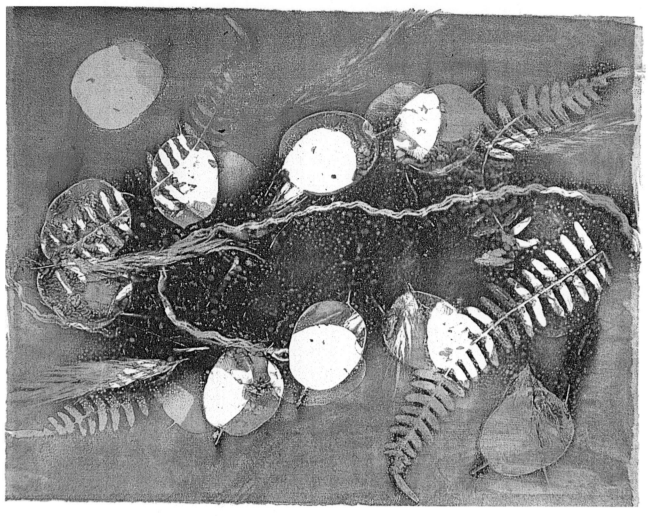

80 *Design printed from ready-made stencils by Maria Mathers*

suitable block-out medium. This is also very time-consuming, and the edges are not as sharp as the results from using cut film.

Greetings cards

In addition to its use for posters, screen printing is an ideal medium for producing greetings cards. Even simple cut-paper stencil designs, such as the shepherd in Fig. 77, can look striking when merely printed in one colour. Because the printing part of the process can be accomplished so quickly, unlike many other print mediums, it provides a practical means of making a dozen or so Christmas cards, for example. If you are not used to editioning

prints, it is also a good way to begin. Being small in size printing cards is a more economic and manageable way to gain experience in editioning. There is also the added incentive of knowing they are going to be of use.

Instead of printing on paper, try using thin card as it is more substantial. This can be bought from any local art shop. Thin card can usually be obtained in any number of subtle shades or bright colours, in addition to the ever-useful white. By starting with a coloured background to print on, you can gain a fuller colour effect with fewer printings. Starting on a coloured background will also lend a more harmonious

effect to the overall result. As an alternative and attractive finish, printing the designs on white paper, then trimming them up and mounting them on toned or coloured card, is easy.

Cut and torn paper stencils is the simplest method to use; it enables you to try out a number of different images to choose from. Yet because of the scale, tusche resist method, or painting directly onto the screen with lacquer etc., can easily be accomplished. The same small screen with, for instance, greetings on it, can be reused each year to save the bother of lettering. In countless ways, printing small images as cards provides an outlet for experimentation.

4 PERSONAL PROFILES

DAVID EVANS AND CO., HOME OF SILK

David Evans, renowned for printed silks, has been established since 1843 (*see Fig. 81*, page 86). Until 1936, textiles were printed solely by the block printing process. From then, screen printing was introduced, and by 1973 block printing was finally phased out. Today it is a highly successful and efficient screen printing company that makes use of automated and computerized processes. At the same time, certain parts of the process are still achieved entirely by hand. Whilst modernizing, exporting and producing orders for prestigious outlets, such as Liberty, it has managed to preserve a friendly, personal image. To one side of the large workshop complex is a small shop where people can buy made-up articles in printed silk, or printed silk by the metre. There is also a *World of Silk* video, and a silk museum. Tours of the silk mills are available by appointment.

Whilst there are studio facilities capable of producing finished designs to order, much of the design work comes in as finished colour art work. From there the colours are separated out and the colour images traced off. Each colour image making up a repeat design is painted by hand onto clear acetate film. A step and repeat camera is then used to duplicate the colour positives exactly into a repeat sequence. From there the repeat strips of film are put onto a repeat engraving machine. They are initially registered by eye. The machine exposes each strip of colour positive, step by step, over a large pre-sensitized screen. The process is by the direct photo stencil method. Once processed and washed out, the stencils are activated, checked, and any pin holes spotted out. The edges of the screen are then finally blocked out.

To start with, the dyes are prepared, mixed and colour matched. This is the most individual area of the large complex of workshops. Both dye and discharge, and acid colours, printed over white, are used. Beyond knowing that, this part of the process remains veiled in trade secrets. Exactly what is used and how it is blended is kept a secret, creating an individual hallmark for David Evans and securing a competitive edge in the world of fabric printing.

The design is printed initially on paper for customer inspection. At this stage the printing is done by hand, often on a printing table with a preheated bed to accelerate the drying time. After this, the screens can be brought into production for printing on silk. The preparation of the silk and the printing process can loosely be divided into nine stages, from the raw material to the finished product.

1 The silk is first boiled out to remove any impurities.

2 Unless the pattern is to be printed on a white background, the lengths of silk are dyed.

3 The silk is then fed into a machine to be dried and stretched.

4 At this stage the lengths of silk need to be perfectly straight for printing. The silk is fed along a bed, where it is pre-stretched to the correct width, and the weave straightened.

5 Now ready for printing, the silk is fastened to long printing beds that extend the length of the building. The printing beds are coated with a permanent adhesive that holds the fabric in place. First one end of the length is ironed into place. The silk is then pulled out straight along the length of the bed, and pressed down onto the adhesive with a wooden stick. A heavy roller is worked along the length of the bed to ensure that the silk is flat and entirely secured ready for printing.

Four different methods of screen printing still exist in the workshops of David Evans: hand printing, although this is being phased out; hand carriage, with set guides; semi-automatic, and automatic.

Contrasts between hand printing and automatic printing

are as wide as you can get. Hand printing is accomplished in the same way, but on a larger scale, as one would print fabrics in small craft workshops or at home. The screen is registered and printed entirely by hand. In contrast to this, automatic printing is achieved, as suggested, entirely by automation. Only the dye and the squeegee need initially to be placed by hand on the screen and printing frame. Then the sizes and printing cycles are fed into a computer.

From then on the printing machine takes over. It travels down the printing bed, stopping at set points to print automatically. At the end of the run, it stops and returns up the bed, ready for starting on the next colour. The used screen merely has to be taken off and the next one replaced. Even cleaning the screen is a simple task, as the screen can be fed through an automatic washer that cleans it in minutes, ready for re-use. Regardless of what method of printing is used, the principle remains the same: each colour required is printed from a separate stencil which is set in perfect alignment to the overall design.

6 After being printed, the silk is taken up and put through a colour fastening machine. As the fabric travels through a layer of steam, the colours are baked and fastened; at the same time, the colours are developed up to their proper appearance. Colours printed by the dye and discharge method can change from sombre tones to vibrant colour.

7 The lengths of silk are then washed to extract any surplus dye. This can be done a number of times, and care is needed to prevent the occurrence of such effects as shadowing.

8 After the final washing, the lengths of silk are placed in the machine used in stage 3. This dries and stretches the fabric.

9 Finally, the finished lengths of silk are put through a finishing stage, which enhances its appearance, giving it a shiny and soft look. At each stage in production the lengths are inspected to ensure the required standard. A final check is made before the finished lengths are ready for dispatch.

MARIA MATHERS

Studied: Digby Stuart College of Education, Stockwell
Taught: art in Kent schools; Victoria Centre for adult education
Work in collections in Norway, USA, France, England and Ireland
At present living and lecturing in Kent

The way most people work is usually influenced as much by the dictates of circumstance as by ideas and personal choice.

Few print makers have anything like totally ideal working environments. Instead, they have to improvise. More often than not, it is basic working conditions, such as available working space and a water supply, that tend to influence how they work.

The printing space used by Maria Mathers, and how it is best organized, is a good illustration of this. Working from an attic room, a flight of stairs away from the nearest water supply, has required a flexible approach to screen printing. Adapting to this problem has meant evolving a system of working that keeps cleaning up and the use of water down to a minimum. In addition to this, the printing space also doubles up as a general painting area.

Yet in dealing with this, Maria has managed to develop a system which is practical and which benefits from cutting out a lot of avoidable drudgery. The general answer to this problem has been to make small editions using cut-paper stencils and water-based inks. By doing this, a number of stencils can be printed consecutively, without washing the screen in between the first light-coloured printings.

Initially a design is made, often with the use of pencils and watercolour. From this a master tracing is made, from which three or four cut-paper

81   *David Evan's silk merchandise*

a

d

e

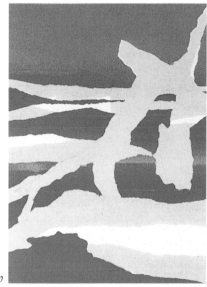

b

c

f

82   Landscape by Maria Mathers. Illustrates the build up of six overprinted stencils (a–f)

stencils are then made. These are designed to be printed using light colours, with warm/cool contrast. By printing only about twelve large, or twenty small, impressions, using water-based inks, these few stencils can be printed consecutively, without stopping, in one session.

After printing the first light colour, excess ink is collected from the screen, and the paper stencil is removed; but the screen is not washed at this stage. Instead, the second stencil is straightaway placed in position over the master copy, new colour is put on the screen, and the printing is then continued. The remnants of the first colour still on the screen, being light, hardly influence the colour of the second printing.

This method of working is continued until the first batch of stencils have been printed. Only then is the screen washed out and left to dry. The process requires a certain amount of organization, so as to be able to work steadily throughout. Too large a time gap in between printing one stencil and the next could result in the ink drying into the screen mesh.

From this stage, the master tracing is dispensed with and the part-printed image is worked from. Two or three stencils are drawn and cut from one of the prints. These are designed to print using darker colours. If one of the colours,

printed from these stencils, happens to print too lightly, the stencil is continually double-printed to compensate for this, and to increase the tone and colour. On occasions the reverse happens and a colour, or the design, becomes too dark. To overcome this, a new stencil is cut and overprinted in a light colour which has white added to it The added white has the effect of lightening that particular area of the print format overall.

Working from the print, rather than continuing to work from the master tracing, can allow more sense of freedom for a print to develop in its own right. Colour, always an important issue, often develops in a different sense to the original design. Sometimes a design will be started by printing a light colour over the entire format area. At other times a colour, with a few shapes blocked out with bits of paper torn at random, will be printed initially. In this way the image is broken into, in much the same way as a random colour can be splashed onto paper before painting, providing confidence and avoiding starting on blank white paper. In addition to using white to adjust dark colours, transparent colours are used throughout.

The equipment used is mainly home-made and very basic — screens and a hinged

baseboard. This operates well with water-based inks, which are made up from Helizarin binder coloured with acrylic paints. Using acrylic colour provides a wide colour option. Working in this manner, with small editions printed without proofing, allows one to take advantage of effects as they happen, often adding to and strengthening them as far as possible.

As an alternative to using cut and torn paper stencils, parts of the images can be made by painting directly onto the screen with screen filler. Wax crayons and candles are also used, often rubbed over textured surfaces placed under the mesh. Experiments with different products are tried out. One such experiment led to the discovery of a particular brand of rubber solution that can be painted on to the screen as a form of resist medium. After lacquer, painted over the screen, has dried, the rubber solution can be rubbed and peeled away. With this improvised method, positive images can be used, while at the same time printing with water-based inks.
(*See Fig. 82*).

CLIVE MILLER

Studied: Bromley College of Art; Royal Academy Schools
Lectured: Medway College of Art; Sheffield College of Art
Exhibited in London, Wales, Nashville (USA), and Holland
At present living and working in Holland

Clive Miller grew up in an environment where print-making was not unusual. Early recollections of his father working coloured his imagination:

I first saw my father working on a light table when I was three years old. It was fascinating to see him working in a dark room, painting on a piece of glass with a light under it. At that age, not understanding the process, the results in these beautiful printed pictures seemed like magic. This influence stayed with me. Later, when taking up painting, my ideal was to produce an image, painted with oils, that looked like a print.

Now a professional artist living in Holland, Clive enjoys working in a variety of mediums. (*See* page 152 for an example of his work.)

As a print-making medium, screen printing offers the widest choice of possible ways in which to work. Clive has always worked in a manner directed towards spontaneous results. The techniques and ideas used are generally straightforward and simple, where the idea will almost immediately show through. Often it has been a question of making a number of alternative images, from which the best results can be selected. It is not surprising, therefore, that the technique of making paper positives for making photo stencils should interest him. Working on layout paper with black Rotring ink and a few brushes, one can quickly build up an image. In addition, it is a simple matter to take the few items required outside and to work directly from subjects, such as landscapes. For a painter, it provides a method of being able to produce print images that are not too divorced from the techniques of drawing and painting. It is independent, to the extent that an image can be made totally independently, and then the help of a print-maker can be sought to process the work and print the results.

In overall terms of painting, it is mainly line and colour that are of most interest to Clive. Finding a relationship between the lines and blocks of colour that will look right is always a problem. In print-making it is impossible to shift the composition around, as in oil painting; you cannot simply scratch out large parts, paint out areas, or move them around. Yet working with paper positives gives a degree of flexibility because the medium is quick to do. It is possible, when not satisfied, to start again and work on until reasonably satisfied that some of the truth of what one was looking for has been established.

Another technique favoured by Clive because of its closeness to painting is that of oil pastel prints. By using this technique, a small series of about six prints can be made, printing any number of colours at the same time. It is more a way of reproducing a drawn coloured image in strictly limited numbers than a way of printing (see oil pastel prints). This technique allows changes to be made to the image during printing, and the printed result can be obtained immediately after the design has been drawn on the screen with oil pastels.

ADVANCED GRAPHICS

Advanced Graphics, a London print studio, is recognized by professional artists and galleries, both in Britain and abroad, for the high quality of its screen print work. It has for a considerable time been among the forerunners of innovative fine art screen printing in Britain. Established in 1967 by Chris Betambeau, it has since moved four times, growing with each move. Although reasonably successful from the start, the real turning point came eighteen months later, with the installation of a giant printing bench. It became possible to produce prints with an image size of up to 150 × 100cm (60 × 40in). Whilst this would have seemed normal practice in the commercial field, it was new to fine art printing, especially in Britain. In collaboration with Bernard Jacobson, director of a high-quality London print gallery, fourteen artists were invited to produce 150 × 100cm (60 × 40in) sized images for editioning. The artists included Patrick Caulfield, John Walker and Eduardo Paolozzi. The venture proved an immediate success, largely helping to gain Advanced Graphics an international reputation.

Printing studios naturally tend to develop their own house style – an individual way of working that provides them with a particular identity. In the case of Advanced Graphics, it has been their attitude towards their artist clientele, rather than a style of printing, that has provided their identity. They hold the belief that the artist and his needs are the most important factors. From the outset of working with a new artist or gallery, they try to adapt and mould themselves around whatever the individual requirements might happen to be. This manner of working, often under pressure to meet new requirements, has led to continual advancement in technique and use of technology.

This was highlighted in *The London Suite*, a portfolio of prints by ten London artists. Published jointly by Advanced Graphics and the artists, it was purposely brought about to open up new areas in screen printing techniques. The resulting freedom in the bold use of colour and drawing greatly expanded the opportunities open to artist and print maker. From the vibrant colour of Albert Irvin, to the rich textures of Mick Moon, and the lively freedom of Gary Wragg, the suite is a virtuoso display of striking imagery and print-making skills alike.

By keeping their options open and not specializing in a particular slot, as is often the case, Advanced Graphics has grown and flourished. At present they edition approximately fifty prints a year. This means that an average of ten to fifteen projects are going on at any one time, some of them taking up to three months to complete. At the same time, the methods and technology used vary considerably: from spontaneously hand-painted glue stencils, used by such artists as Trevor Jones, to trichromatic stencils using the latest in laser scanning technology. Yet, despite the need for organization and occasional pressure, the working atmosphere in the studio appears friendly and relaxed. Amidst the chaos of drying racks and paraphernalia, the operation runs smoothly under the watchful eyes of Chris Betambeau and Bob Saich (who became a partner in 1977).

From the artist's point of view, the working environment comes possibly as close to the ideal situation as practicality allows. It is certainly flexible enough to suit most needs. The amount of time an artist might spend in the studio varies considerably. Some prefer to approach the studio with a finished painting; after discussing how best the image can be interpreted, and the costs involved, they will leave it entirely in the hands of the printer, only to see the finished proof at the end. Other artists might wish to visit from time to time to see what progress is being made. Artists like John Swanson prefer to work in the studio daily, making stencils and colour decisions etc. throughout the development of the print. John Hoyland and Trevor Jones have used the studio to produce series of mono prints, developed from spontaneously hand-painted glue stencils.

Some artists arrive with a set of stencils and colours, having already proofed the image themselves. Being unable to produce facsimile editioning

83   *From design stage . . . to finished print with Advanced Graphics and John Swansan*

84   *Silk craft centre; photograph courtesy of David Evans*

(not having the facilities or room for long runs), they prefer to have this done for them by Advanced Graphics.

The company is soon to be moving to a new location in Creekside, Deptford/Greenwich, and new ventures are already envisaged. With space available, there are thoughts of acquiring a large hydraulic press for making mono prints. The tactile printed effects can be quite different from anything else. As the print is released from the press, the ink drags up into specialized effects. The results can be further enhanced by unusual additives, such as fish scales. Advanced Graphics hope to combine screen printing with these results.

JOHN SWANSON

Solo Exhibitions 1987–1989: Museum of History and Art, Ontario CA; Museum of Art, Science and Industry, Bridgeport, CT; Bazaar del Mundo Gallery, San Diego, CA; Bergsma Gallery (travelling exhibition of prints) **Collections in** Brooklyn Museum; Smithsonian Museum of American Art; Bibliothèque Nationale, Paris; Tate Gallery, London; Victoria and Albert Museum, London

John Swanson did not paint until the age of thirty. Then, without any formal art training, but through experimentation and research, he began to develop a means of visual expression that continues to progress in a highly individual and personal way. His work can best be described as figurative-narrative of a naïve character, emphasizing fine detail and richness of colour. Influences in both painting and print-making have ranged from medieval painting to Islamic miniatures, and from Russian iconography to Mexican muralists.

In the late Sixties he experimented with designing and printing art posters. The designs, printed in simple flat colours, usually incorporated lettering and were popular at the time. Easily accessible, they provided a means of reaching a wider and larger audience. He continued printing his own work until 1975, when the opportunity of financial backing enabled him to have the printing undertaken by fine art print workshops. Working in collaboration with a master printer meant a broadening in the possibilities of image-making. Different techniques, expert technical advice and improved equipment were available. More separate colours and detail work could be used and accurately aligned. Since 1975, John has worked with six different print workshops, four in the USA and two in England.

Unlike many contemporary artists who, after a consultation, leave the printing in the hands of a print workshop, John works throughout the printing in very close collaboration with the master printer. Each small stage of the printing is usually discussed and the possibilities considered. A fine balance is drawn between artist and printer, between the intended quality of a particular image and the technical input required to achieve it. With possibly forty to fifty separate stencils being used on an image, an overall strategy is a key factor to success. For instance, several recent large prints were so elaborate that they needed to be printed a section at a time. In this way it was possible to achieve a better degreee of accuracy in the registration of coloured detail.

At the time of writing, John is working in collaboration with Advanced Graphics in London. He started working with Chris Betambeau in 1976, and since 1985 he has returned each year to work on a project with him. In three months he is to complete two print projects, each of which will be built up using forty-plus separate stencils. Due to the complexity of the images, smaller paintings are made. The initial strategy, is to produce a series of posterized trichromatic stencils from transparencies from the paintings. However, the colours printed are not necessarily trichromatic.

With a few stencils printed in light colours, a good basis for registration is established, and an outline master tracing is produced from the print. Hand-drawn and painted flat colour stencils are then made and printed. Other trichromatic stencils are used in between the hand-drawn ones. During the process, possibly fifteen colours will be added using trichromatic stencils.

To add further detail and textural effects, fine hand-drawn stencils are overprinted in white. Then numerous other hand-drawn and painted stencils are made and overprinted. Some are printed in transparent blends of colour to further enrich the image; others add textures and fine detail which sharpen up the imagery. The whites used earlier soften down, disappearing in part, in the matrix of richly overlaid colours.

In achieving this, Chris Betambeau takes overall charge, from a procedural print-making point of view, while Dave Wood, a master printer, mixes the colours and does the printing. With so many colours and stencils used, the images are only proofed to a partly-finished state. The finished image is finally developed during editioning.
(*See Fig. 85*, page 94).

LIZ HOWE

Studied: Goldsmiths College, London
Taught: art and print-making in London; Kent; Trinidad
At present living and teaching in Kent

Liz Howe first became interested in screen printing whilst at Goldsmiths College. Since then, she has run print workshops in schools and youth clubs, etc. She believes that screen printing is an ideal activity for getting children interested in art. It helps them to develop both practical and intellectual skills, as well as a sense of visual awareness. Equally important is that it is fun to do. Because the printed results are produced mechanically, unlike in painting or drawing, they eliminate personal clumsiness.

Through children's eyes, the printed results look smart. Both talented and less-able children can excel in screen printing and be equally pleased by the results – results that can be achieved in a short time by using simple means. Children who think of themselves as 'non-drawers' readily become involved in tearing and cutting paper stencils. The most simple image, when screen printed, can look very sophisticated and professional. Printed results can be seen to work like magic. Finished images look so crisp and clear, with flat areas of vibrant colour, that as a child raises the screen for the first time, he or she is instantly thrilled at this easily-achieved result.

Screen printing is both simple and economic to establish and use in schools. Oddments of equipment needed, such as screens, can be easily made. Cotton organdie makes an ideal screen fabric for school use. It is reasonably cheap and, with care, can be reused numerous times. Strips of card can be used in place of squeegees, which are expensive. For printing on paper, ready-mix paints work well. They can be used directly from the plastic bottles to produce a range of vibrant colour that is effective when overprinted.

From the children's point of view, screen printing can be put to good practical uses. Printed tee-shirts are always popular. For printing, they need only to be stretched over a drawing board with paper padding underneath. Cartridge paper, rather than newsprint, works more effectively for stencil making. The extra thickness of cartridge paper provides the thicker ink deposit needed in fabric printing. Printex binder and inks, specially made for fabric printing, are economic for use in schools and easy to print with. Pop star images, names and slogans – favourites with all groups of children – can easily be cut as stencils.

85   Circus Bicyclist *by John Swanson*

86　X-ray Skull *Series by Graham Williams*

87　Recycled Parts *by Graham Williams*

88　*Results of fabric painting by children working with Liz Howe*

Younger children work better with random designs. Two or three simple cut or torn newsprint stencils are made. These can then be moved around on a sheet of black paper to decide how they can best be positioned for printing. With no rubbing out, as in drawing, this always seems an enjoyable activity. The printing promotes a sense of team work, with pairs of children working towards a finished result. One holds down the screen while the other prints, and so on.

Older children are able to work in a more reasoned way. They usually build up three colours as simple overprinted blocks, then look for a more deliberate stencil design incorporating linear detail. The effect of this usually seems to add icing to the cake.

The most popular item of equipment is the light box. Used by children of all ages, it helps them to develop a sense of design and colour. Colours painted on thin paper show up well under the intensity of light. The possibilities of overprinted colour can be instantly seen, as the various colour shapes are rearranged in overlapping patterns. (*See* page 95).

GRAHAM WILLIAMS

Colleges: Sheffield Polytechnic School of Art and Design; Liverpool Polytechnic School of Art and Design; Manchester Polytechnic School of Art and Design; Slade School of Fine Art; Wimbledon School of Art **Exhibited:** 1987 Hardware Gallery, London; Audun Gallery, London; 1988 Royal Festival Hall, London; University of Surrey Gallery; University of Newcastle Gallery **At present** living and print-making in London

During a spate of regularly travelling on London Underground, Graham Williams became interested in the surroundings. Often struck by the multi-layered torn posters, with their randomly-juxtaposed images and general state of decay, he decided to look for some sort of equivalent in print-making terms. Two of the features of this kind of imagery were the variation of placing, and how different images were when defaced. Rather than make facsimile print editions, his aim became to produce prints with permutations of the elements used. It is a system where the same components are used to build up a series of mono-prints. The imagery may look similar, but no two prints are the same. Each one is unique, much the same way as in painting.

Graham Williams describes the process he uses in the following way.

The prints are not planned too carefully in advance. They evolve through the printing process, each one being built up separately. In this way the printing process itself becomes a creative act. The technique used is fairly simple. A repertoire of about six stencil images is available at any one time. Possibly fifty sheets of paper are in use, and any image is printed any number of times, in any position, on any sheet and in any colour. This is not done in an entirely random way. After a while, one will decide that enough use has been made out of the stencil images and they will be changed. This process continues until the prints are finished. This decision is arrived at intuitively. When prints are finished, they are removed from the stock on the rack and are substituted with blank sheets of paper.

In making these prints, Graham often prefers to use found objects which are capable of reproducing their own image. Discarded rubber car mats are a particular favourite. Apart from the use of ready-made stencils, there is an allegorical suggestion to much of his work. Elements such as skulls, music and quotations are often used with images as diverse as Chinese paper cuts and X-rays. (*See* page 95).

5 MORE ADVANCED TECHNIQUES

PHOTOGRAPHIC STENCILS

Within recent years there has been continual advancement in the development of photographic emulsions and films. The products available today are very reliable, durable and work well for high-quality close-registration colour printing. They are also indispensable for designs requiring fine drawn or painted detail. What is equally important is that they are very straightforward and easy to use. Once the stencil-making procedure has been fully understood, with a little practice this method of stencil-making is very easy. Difficulties should occur only rarely. Provided that the procedure has been carried out correctly, the stencils should be robust, standing up well to use and lengthy editioning.

The photo stencil process

The photo stencil process works due to the use of light-sensitive material that hardens when exposed to ultraviolet light. This material is marketed in two different forms. In liquid form, referred to as the 'direct method', it can be pre-coated onto the screen before being processed. As film, the 'indirect method', it is already coated on a temporary acetate backing. The film is processed before being transferred to the screen.

For both methods, a light-proof positive image is made on a sheet of clear acetate. This is placed over the light-sensitive coating. A timed exposure to ultraviolet light is then made. The ultraviolet light hardens only the exposed parts of the film coating: the areas of emulsion concealed beneath the positive image remain soft. A simple developer is then used to further harden the exposed parts of the film stencil. On washing the emulsion with warm water, the soft areas of film emulsion start to dissolve, finally disappearing to leave a negative stencil that is the exact opposite of the positive image. When printed, the result will show a facsimile likeness to the original positive image.

Direct and indirect photo stencils

Both direct and indirect methods of making photo stencils have various advantages. The direct method, with sensitized liquid coated onto the screen, then processed, is capable of greater wear and is cheaper to produce. However, the indirect method of photo stencils produces excellent definition. This is due to good mesh bridging. Because the film emulsion rests on the surface of the mesh, but is not part of it, it is not interrupted by the weave of the fabric (*Fig. 89*). This also enables finer detail to be printed. As the stencils are not imbedded in the mesh, they can be removed more readily. Direct photo stencils often require a high-pressure hose to remove them successfully.

Finally, during most of the processing of indirect photo stencils, one has only to cope with the actual size of the stencil, not the larger screen size. When considering available space and apparatus size, this can make a difference. For these reasons, only the full procedure for the indirect photo stencil method will be dealt with here.

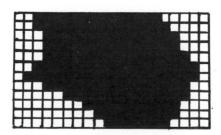

89a *Diagram of screen mesh and direct photo stencil, highly magnified. The stencil, incorporated into the screen fabric, has uneven edges due to the interruption of the mesh*

b *Diagram of screen mesh and indirect photo stencil, highly magnified. The stencil is independent of the mesh, taking on a more clear-cut form*

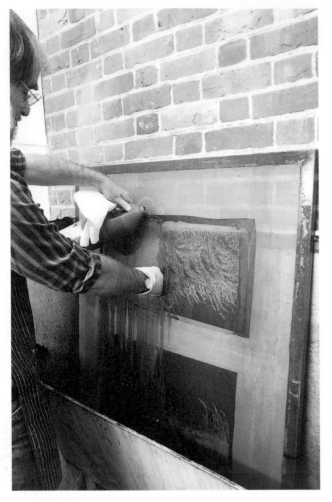

90 *Clean off the stencil with bleach*

91 *Clean the screen with two pads of cloth and general purpose screen wash*

Making an indirect photo stencil: preparation

Apart from large items such as the exposure unit, washout unit and printing down frame, there are a number of smaller items that you will require. These are listed below.

Items required for making the stencil
Scissors
Photographic stencil film
A and B developer
(1pt) Measure
Storage jar
Plastic developing dish
2 paper clips
Large spoon or palette knife
Rubber roller
Newspaper
Bottle of screen stop out

Screen filler
Short length of squeegee blade
Small brush
Parcel tape

Items for cleaning and preparing the screen
Household bleach
General purpose screen wash
Cleaning cloths
Household cream cleaner
Rubber gloves

Cleaning and preparing the screen

In order for the photo stencil to work well, the screen must first be thoroughly cleaned and degreased. If this is not properly carried out, the film stencil will not have good adhesion to the screen, and

parts of the stencil could become loose during printing, spoiling the finished printed result.

Correct cleaning procedure

1 Using cold water, thoroughly hose away the screen filler surrounding the photo stencil. Then carefully pour household bleach along the top edge of the stencil, rubbing it over the surface of the stencil with a cleaning tissue. After repeated attempts, the stencil will dissolve (*Fig. 90*). As a cautionary measure, only attempt this in a well-ventilated room. Keep a flow of water running in the bottom of the washout unit, or sink, to stop a build-up of bleach. Also, wear a pair of rubber gloves when doing this, and do it at arms' length to avoid splashes of bleach and fumes. When the stencil has thoroughly dissolved, gently hose down the screen with water.

2   Stand the screen against a wall to dry.

3   When the screen is dry, fold two cleaning cloths into pads and soak them in general purpose screen wash. Holding a pad in either hand, start to clean the screen (*Fig. 91*). By holding the pads against either side of the mesh, work them across the surface in a series of circular motions. When ink-stained, remake the pads to use clean areas of the cloth. After this, repeat the procedure using two newly-soaked pads. Ensure you clean the entire surface of the screen thoroughly.

4   Starting from the top of the screen, hose across the top of the mesh with a strong jet of cold water in a series of parallel motions. As you work across and down the screen you will see the residue of ink and cleaner disappearing.

5   Check the screen for any remaining spots of stencil or screen stop out. These should be removed with bleach and the screen lightly hosed down with cold water afterwards.

6   The cleaned screen will need to be degreased. This will

ensure that the stencil adheres well. Also, the smooth surface of the monofilament polyester mesh will need to be slightly roughened, to provide better purchase for the film stencil. This is called 'putting tooth' on the mesh. Household cream cleaner will act as a degreasing agent, at the same time scouring the surface of the mesh sufficiently to roughen it.

Balance the screen at an angle to a wall. Squirt cream cleaner on the back of the screen. Then fold a cleaning cloth into a pad. Work this firmly across and down the screen surface in a series of circular motions (*Fig. 92*). To ensure that you have covered the entire screen surface with this treatment, work the pad up and down the screen in overlapping motions. This treatment should both degrease the screen and 'put tooth' on it. Finally, rinse the cream cleaner from the screen with a jet of cold water. As you do so, you will notice that the water, no longer repelled by grease, gives the screen a clearer appearance.

This combination of bleach for removing photo stencils, and cream cleaner for degreasing the screen and putting tooth on it, is not entirely orthodox procedure. It was shown to me by the printer from who I bought my equipment. It has always worked perfectly well for me, as it did for him. Yet

92   *Using cream cleaner on the screen*

other printers do not favour this use of materials. The alternative is to use brand name stencil remover, degreasing agent and abrasive material, obtainable from a screen printing supplier.

Regardless of products used, the degreasing part of the procedure should always be done just prior to making the photo stencil. Screens degreased days before use will become impregnated with dust and could become greasy. After degreasing a screen, lean it against a wall in readiness to accept the washed-out stencil.

93   Cut out the photographic stencil film

94   *Printing down frame, from top to bottom: plate glass sheet, positive, shiny* side up; photo film, shiny side up; sheet of newspaper

Procedure for making an indirect photographic stencil

1   Remove the film roll from the container in the safety of indirect daylight or artificial light. While the film is sensitive to ultraviolet light and should not be exposed to direct sunlight, shaded conditions and yellow light will not affect it. There is no need to attempt this procedure in a scarcely-lit room.

Carefully unroll part of the film, emulsion side facing upwards, on a flat working surface. Avoid creasing the film: creases could affect the final adhesion of the film to the screen. Place the positive over the rolled-out film, allowing approximately a 5cm (2in) border of film to overlap the positive. Use scissors to cut the required shape of the film (*Fig. 93*). Reroll the unused film and return it to the container. When not in use, store the film in a cold dry place and keep the top tightly screwed on.

2   Place the film and positive in the printing down frame (*Fig. 94*). The positive should be directly under the glass sheet and the film beneath the positive. Both film and positive should be shiny side upwards — in other words, the shiny surface of the film backing and the back of the positive face upwards.

95   *The positive and film are placed in the printing down frame*

96 Lilies *by Maria Mathers*

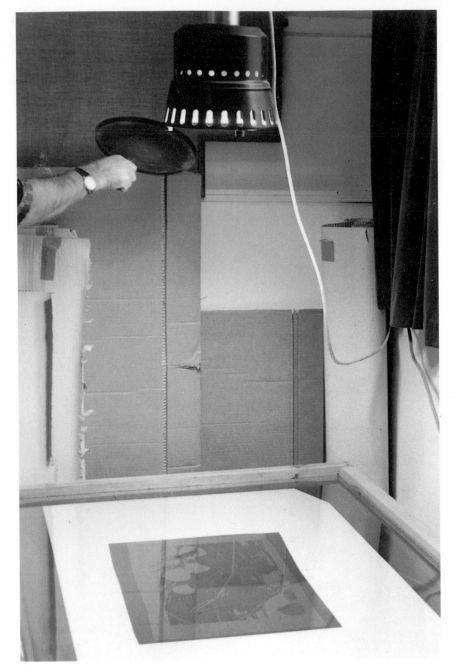

97   *Expose the film to the mercury vapour lamp*

3   With the shield in place, turn on the mercury vapour lamp for 5 minutes to warm up. If using a vacuum printing down frame, switch on the vacuum pump at the same time, and press on the plate glass. This will ensure that all the air is expelled from the printing down frame, to give the best possible contact between positive and film during exposure. If using a glass sheet with foam rubber backing, ensure that the glass is correctly weighted down. In both cases, wipe over the top of the glass to remove any dust particles.

4   Then, with the lamp warmed to full brightness and a vacuum created, remove the shield from the lamp and expose the film for the correct length of time (see texposure times) (*Fig. 97*).

5   At the end of the exposure time, replace the shield over the lamp and switch off the exposure unit. Turn off the vacuum pump and open the valve to allow air to re-circulate back into the printing down frame.

6   Remove the positive and film from the printing down frame. Place the film in the developing tray, emulsion side upwards. Stir the pre-mixed developer thoroughly using a palette knife, then pour the developer over the film. Make sure it covers the entire film surface (*Fig. 98*). Use your fingers (rubber gloves can be worn) to agitate the developer lightly over the film surface. Develop for the correct time, as indicated on the packet.

7   Hold the film by two corners, with the emulsion side facing you, above the tray. Allow excess developer to drain off into the tray. Place the developed film against the back of the washout unit, secured by two paper clips at the top. The emulsion side of the film should still be facing towards you. Return the developer to the storage jar.

8   With a shower attachment, sprinkle hand-warm water over the emulsion side of the film (*Fig. 99*). The soft parts of the stencil, previously shielded by the positive, should dissolve and start to wash away. Continue to sprinkle warm water over the entire surface of

98   *Ensure the film is covered in developer*

the film, not just the parts with the image. A certain amount of colour should wash away from the entire film surface. Carry on until the colour stops washing out. Closely inspect the stencil to ensure that the open spaces have thoroughly washed away leaving a clear sharp-edged stencil. When this is done, turn off the water heater and sprinkle cold water gently over the entire film to harden, or 'chill', the emulsion.

9   Take hold of the film by the top corners, holding the emulsion side away from you. Position the film in the centre of a prepared screen. The emulsion side of the film, held away from you, should be resting against the mesh. Once positioned, the wetness of the film will hold it in place. Should a fold or crease appear on the surface when positioning the film, gently peel it from the screen and try again.

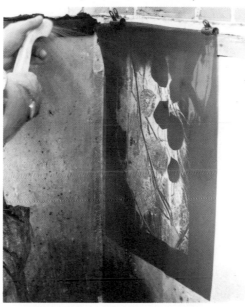

99   *Shower warm water over the emulsion side of the film*

10   Place three sheets of clean newspaper on a smooth flat working surface. Lower the screen onto the paper, with the film resting against the paper. Place three further sheets of newspaper over the top of the mesh.

11   Gently roll across the top of the newspaper-covered mesh using a rubber roller (*Fig. 100*). This part of the process will remove excess moisture from the stencil. Whilst the stencil

100   *Gently roll across the top of the newspaper*

101 *Remove the final sheet from the stencil*

needs to be secured against the mesh, it is not the intention to force the stencil emulsion into the weave. Excess pressure would only result in breaks in the stencil where the mesh has cut into it, or distortions which could ruin the printed results. Roll from the centre of the stencil outwards – this will avoid any creases forming in the stencil. Remove the two wet sheets of newspaper closest to the screen, one above the screen and one underneath. Use firm light pressure to roll across the newspaper covering the screen in a series of movements away from you. Then, to ensure that you cover the entire stencil area, roll across the surface with movements from side to side. As before, remove two more sheets of newspaper. Roll across the screen for a third time, backwards and forwards and side to side, and remove the final sheets of newspaper (*Fig. 101*). The stencil should now be fully secured to the mesh.

12 Stand the screen against a wall, with the film stencil facing towards you. Drying times will vary with the room temperature. Gentle warmth from a fan heater, placed a distance away from the screen, will shorten the drying time. As the photo stencil dries on the screen, the backing layer changes colour, lightening as it is released from the film stencil emulsion. When the entire surface of the acetate backing has changed to a lighter colour, indicating that is is released from the film, it can be peeled away from the screen. To do this, catch up a corner edge of the backing sheet with your

finger nail, then slowly and carefully peel back the acetate to reveal the finished stencil. A word of caution: make amply sure that the stencil has fully dried before removing the backing, otherwise parts of the film emulsion may come away with the acetate.

13 With the backing sheet removed, check the stencil against a window for pin holes. Paint over any holes in the stencil with a small brush and screen stop out (*Fig. 102*). Leave to dry.

14 With the stencil facing upwards, lower the screen onto a flat working surface. Pour some screen filler onto the margin of the screen. Using the short length of stencil blade, spread the filler across the screen margins to overlap the edges of the stencil. If ink leaks

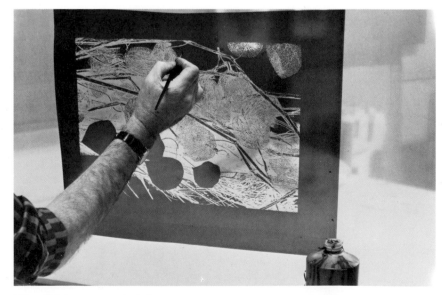

102 *Paint over any pin holes*

103   Reclining Figure *by Nicholas Bristow*

104   Figure and Lilies *by Nicholas Bristow*

105   Figure and Tulips *by Nicholas Bristow*

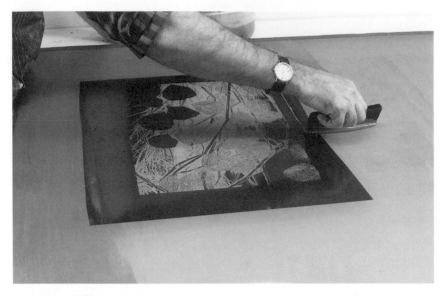

106   *Spread filler across the screen margins*

107   *Tape round the edges of the screen*

during printing, it usually happens along the edges of the photo stencil, between film and screen filler. To avoid this, fully cover up the edges of the stencil.

15   When dry, hold the screen up to the light to ensure that the entire border areas have been covered. Attend to any missed parts, or pin holes, with additional screen filler.

16   When dry, tape round the edges of the screen using parcel tape (*Fig. 107*).

The screen is now ready for printing. Should a small leak occur during printing, it can be quickly stopped by patching the back of the screen with parcel tape, or masking tape.

Having photo stencils made for you

While the photo stencil process is an excellent method of working and means of providing detailed imagery and precision printing, the equipment needed and space required for making stencils may be beyond your scope. But this does not necessarily mean

that using photo stencils is outside your scope. It is simply a question of finding an alternative means of getting them made for you.

In every large town, there should be at least one screen printer, operating a small business producing poster and general advertising. If not disturbed at an inopportune moment, most small printers are particularly helpful and should be able to process a photo stencil, from your positive, onto your own screen for a small cost.

If you do not have the appropriate frame and mesh for this to be done, you still have one alternative: you can design an image which will rely on just one detailed photographic stencil, which would finally be printed in a dark colour or tone (*Fig. 108*). This final dark image could work in the 'key' sense of adding definition, detail and texture overall to the previously-printed colours.

Design an image, make the stencils and print a small edition yourself, up to the final stage of the 'key' image stage. This can be made with any number of colours, using cut paper stencils and water- or oil-based inks. Secure one of the prints to a drawing board, with a sheet of acetate on top. Make the positive needed for the final stencil.

Take the positive and printed edition along to your local

108　Fort Gardens *by Maria Mathers. A series of cut and torn stencils was first printed using water-based inks. A key image photo stencil was then made, and overprinted, from an acetate positive by a commercial printer*

screen printer. Using your positive, he should be able to process the final image onto one of his screens. Agree with him on the colour to be printed. Between jobs, at a slack time, he should be able to overprint your small edition with the final colour. The cost that you will be charged for either processing a photo stencil onto your own screen, or to use his screen to overprint the final colour, should not be prohibitive. If you were to compare this cost with the expense of setting up and maintaining your own photo stencil system, it would very likely seem an economical way of working.

Designs for indirect stencils

The advent of the indirect stencil, with its property of perfect mesh bridging, has led to a period of boundless scope in screen printing. This, coupled with improved meshes and inks, now allows the widest range of marks, lines and textures to be faithfully reproduced. With the use of correct products, a certain amount of practice and commonsense, all but the most minute detail can be achieved.

PHOTOGRAPHIC POSITIVES

Photographic positives, usually referred to as photo positives, are what the name implies — 'positive' images. From these, exact negative photo stencils are made. When printed, the stencils revert the images back to facsimiles of the original positives.

Acetate: for drawn and painted images

The material on which positive designs are made should meet three main requirements. Firstly, it must be transparent, to allow ultraviolet light to pass through the unworked areas in order to harden the sensitized film emulsion. Secondly, it should be rigid and impervious to moisture, otherwise the design would shrink or stretch with atmospheric changes, affecting the alignment of the various stencils. Thirdly, the surface

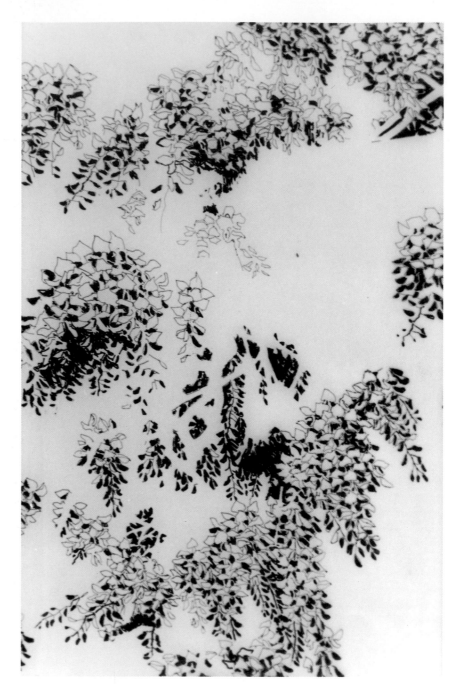

109 *Delicate line work and detail using Rotring black drawing ink*

must be receptive to the mediums used in making the design. To meet all of these requirements, sheets of acetate are used. There is a variety of products available, some more transparent than others. Brand names like Kodatrace, Permatrace, Selectatrace and Draftfilm are commonly used. They can usually be bought by the sheet or roll.

Whilst the surfaces of these products may seem harsh in comparison to paper, they are nevertheless capable of carrying a wide variety of marks, lines and textures. The most important factor in painting or drawing an image is that you make it lightproof. Failure to achieve this would more than likely result in a poorly-defined stencil.

Rapidograph, or Rotring black drawing ink, while providing density, can be used for broadly-painted areas, delicate line work and textural detail (*Fig. 109*). They are reliable mediums with which to work, but are slow drying, especially when used broadly.

Red photo opaque, which is a paste-like substance the colour of red oxide, can be watered down and is good for broad areas. It is opaque and dries to an even thickness, usually making a second coat unnecessary. However, in certain conditions, photo opaque seems to absorb moisture and can turn tacky.

Chinagraph pencils provide adequate density of tone and can be used for adding variety of line work and textures, etc. Care needs to be taken in storing the positives as Chinagraph marks smudge easily. There are other mediums that can be used, such as black printing ink.

Ink positives, especially those with large solid areas, usually take a long time to dry completely, as the ink does not dry partly by absorption as it does when worked on paper. When dry, the density of a drawing can look misleading. Drawings and paintings tend to look more opaque than they really are, and even the strongest-looking drawing will need checking for density. Hold the positive up to a window, or over a light box, and make a note of any lighter-toned areas. These will need a second coat of ink or photo opaque.

110   The Shepherds *by John Swanson*   111   The Conductor *by John Swanson*

112   *A variety of different textures and reversed-out line work*

Red masking film

Red masking film can be used for either hand-cut stencils or hand-cut photo positives. It consists of a thin red layer of light-proof material adhered to a clear acetate backing. Although impervious to ultraviolet light, it is still reasonably transparent. A traced design, or ink positive, can clearly be seen through its surface; so too can a positive cut from red masking film. An image is made by lightly cutting round the shapes of a design, using a sharp knife like a scalpel or craft knife. The surrounding areas, negative parts of the design, are then carefully peeled away from the acetate backing. Straight edges can be cut with the aid of a metal rule. Any mistakes can be rectified by resticking down a piece of previously-lifted red material, and recutting that part of the design. This may look untidy, but should work as well as the rest of the design.

This type of stencil will have the general appearance of a cut paper stencil. However, it is possible to work to designs of far greater intricacy and detail. The edges of shapes made with masking film are sharper and the shapes more accurate, and because of the backing, any number of small free-standing shapes can be used.

Unlike with paper stencils, the screen can be cleaned whilst still leaving the stencil intact to be reprinted. This means that different colours can be tried out at a proofing stage, after which the screen can be stored indefinitely, or until the edition is printed. Produced as photo stencils, cut-out red mask images will withstand the heavy wear resulting from editioning up to a few hundred prints.

Positives cut from masking film are often used in the initial stages of making a print. The first few colours, usually designed to print in simple broad areas of light colours, can quickly and accurately be cut from sheets of red masking film. Apart from taking less time, there is a saving on drying time. Cut positives can be overlayed on a light box, and worked with as soon as they are finished.

Ensuring correct registration when making positives

An important factor when making a set of positives is to ensure correct alignment throughout. Regardless of colour and design, the end result will only be as good as the registration allows. Poor registration invariably produces poor results. To ensure against such events, a workable procedure for obtaining the best possible alignment of stencils needs to be set out and kept to. In this way one can concentrate on such issues as painting, drawing and design, with the

113   *The clear-cut quality of red masking film positives is ideally suited to screen printing*

reassurance that the end results will print in agreement with each other. There are doubtless various ways of ensuring this. The following is a description of the method that I use.

Procedure for making a set of hand-drawn and painted photo positives

1   From the original design, make a master tracing on a sheet of layout paper. Using a steel straightedge, draw a clear thin pencilled line along the bottom and right-hand side of the traced design. Use a set square to ensure that the two lines are set at right angles to each other.

2   Cut out the pieces that you need, approximately 1.2cm ($\frac{1}{2}$in) larger than the design, from acetate drawing film. Using a steel straightedge and scalpel, cut straight edges at right angles to each other, along the bottom and right-hand side of the acetate sheets.

3   Tape the master tracing onto a light box; failing this use a drawing board. Place a sheet of acetate over this, ensuring that the bottom and right-hand edges of the acetate are in true alignment with the corresponding ruled lines on the master tracing. Carefully tape down the acetate.

4   With Rotring, or similar, ink, draw and paint in the areas you intend to print in a

particular colour, with this positive.

5   Remove the first completed positive, leaving it in a safe place to dry. Line up and secure the second sheet of acetate. Draw in the second colour positive with Rotring ink. Continue in the same manner until you have the required number of positives. As a further aid, finished dry positives can be taped over the tracing. This will give some idea as to how the design is progressing, and will act as an indicator, suggesting the build-up of overprinted colours.

6   Once the required number of positives have been made, carefully tape them down, with small pieces of masking tape, to a light box, or sheet of plate glass. As you tape each positive down, use the bottom and right-hand edges to bring them into perfect alignment. Check each stencil as it is aligned for

accuracy. If the registration can be improved by moving it slightly, do so and tape it down in that position.

7   When all the positives have been taped down and the registration checked, the edges can be trimmed. Place a steel straightedge along one side of the assembled positives, allowing enough of the edges to protrude to ensure that a small amount of each positive will be cut away. Carefully cut along the edge with a Stanley knife, making sure you cut through all of the assembled positives. In the same way, recut the remaining three sides of the positives. You will now have a set of identical-sized positives. When the photo stencils made from these are realigned during the final printing, they should be in exact agreement.

114 *and* 115 *Drawings made with various brushes and Rotring ink on layout paper*

PAPER POSITIVES AND SPONTANEOUS DRAWN IMAGES

To achieve anything approaching an entirely spontaneous result in screen printing would seem a difficult task. Even at best the technique seems a long and drawn-out procedure when compared to, for instance, painting. One cannot just design and print a few lines and patches of colour in several minutes, as in painting. The whole process takes time. Fortunately, time is not a crucial factor in pursuing a majority of ideas. Yet there are occasions when time and spontaneity form a central role – ideas, for instance where qualities like movement, mood

and atmosphere are the uppermost ingredients.

Figures in movement, where a gestural image is needed, could seem very stilted, adapted to a series of slowly-produced drawings, or cut-out stencils. To convey something like the fleeting impression of a dance movement, a method enabling one to encapsulate the idea quickly is required (*Figs 114 and 115*). A technique that comes close to achieving this is known as the 'paper positive' method.

Paper positives

Drawings produced in black ink on layout paper can be used directly as positives for photo stencils. The method works on the principle that oily paper is less impervious to light, and thus more light is allowed through. Therefore, a drawing previously soaked in an oily

substance will become sufficiently-transparent to allow enough light to pass through it to form a photo stencil. Paraffin is the usually-recommended substance to achieve this. While paraffin works effectively, it also leaves an oily residue on the paper. For this reason, I prefer to use white spirit. Although more difficult to use, due to evaporation, the original drawing is not ruined in the process.

Procedure for making a paper positive

1   Produce a drawing on a sheet of layout paper, using black Rotring ink.

2   When dry, check the density of the ink drawing on a light box, or by holding it up to a window. Any parts of the drawing that seem light will

116 *Tusche, glue and tusche resist stencil*

117 Tractor *by Moss Evans*

need a second coat of ink. Pay particular attention to large areas of ink.

3 When completely dry, use a clean rag soaked in white spirit to wipe over the back of the drawing. Thoroughly soak the back of the drawing with white spirit. Afterwards, wipe off excess liquid using a clean dry rag.

4 The paper positive can now be processed in the same way as an acetate positive.

The only differences in using a paper positive instead of an acetate one are a loss of minute detail and texture and a possible difference of exposure time needed. With, for instance, a gestural drawing, any loss of detail, or texture, would be so slight as to go unnoticed. With timing the exposure, I have always kept to the same time as for acetate positives. It is, however, prudent to initially produce a test strip with a range of slightly longer exposure times.

Benefits and uses of paper positives
Paper positives are easy to use and provide a free, uncomplicated way of working. They are also very cost-effective. Drawing on layout paper is fractional in expense to working on acetate. When working on paper, one can easily afford to be generous. It is possible to make large numbers of quick studies from which to make a final selection.

From the point of view of working, the surface of layout paper is more receptive than the rigid quality of acetate. Likewise, it is easier to evaluate the quality of a drawing against the white of the paper. Yet layout paper is thin enough to overlay a drawing with fresh paper and produce a facsimile, with mistakes remedied, or variations tried out.

A sensible use of the paper positive method is to use it for making a key image drawing. This can then be implemented with a few simple stencils as back-up tones and colours. The tusche resist method is as good a way as any of achieving this. The two methods of working are quite compatible, each seeming to support the other. The design holds together rather like a pen and wash drawing, the looseness of the tusche resist stencils adding bulk and colour in a way similar to watercolour washes, while the paper positive image supplies structure and a sense of delineation to the design overall.

Experiments with ready-made paper positives

The ever-increasing wealth of printed paraphernalia freely available these days can be used to good effect. Much of it, printed on thin paper, can be used as a source of ready-made paper positives. Soaked in paraffin and processed, they can be used in a printed collage sense. Even paper printed on both sides can be used to good effect — the random patterns of shapes and textures often leading to unusual results.

COUNTERCHANGE

The use of counterchange can add vitality to an otherwise quite ordinary design. It can create a sense of variety, especially in monochromatic designs, or those employing few printings and colour. By reversing the tonal changes, dark against light then light against dark, a quality of enrichment can be obtained. Producing a light image against a dark background is easy when broad areas are needed. Simple large shapes can be effectively painted around.

This is not possible, however, when reversed, light-coloured, drawing and detail is needed. Then, the best option is to use a form of resist medium. The reversed drawing is first made with a resist medium, such as a sharpened candle. Then the whole area is painted over in black ink with a broad brush. The greasy nature of the candle-waxed drawing repels the ink, leaving the drawn design untouched by the ink (*Fig. 118*). Candle wax resist is suitable for creating robust drawing and a variety of textured effects. However, it is

118 *Counterchange using a resist medium*

unsuitable for fine detail work and precision drawing. Positives incorporating light-toned detail are best made with the use of masking fluid.

The use of art masking fluid for counterchange photo positives

Masking fluid, a product associated with watercolour painting and graphic art, can be used to achieve a wide range of counterchange effects. It is a milky-looking fluid, obtainable in white or yellow colour, and can be applied with either a brush or a pen. In its liquid state, it is water-soluble. However, it is quick-drying and care should be taken that brushes are rinsed out immediately after use. When dry, it has a rubbery consistency. Unlike candle wax, it can be rubbed and pulled away from a finished design to leave a clearly-defined negative image. Always shake the bottle

well before use and remember to keep the top screwed on.

Start by painting and drawing in the parts of the positive that you intend to leave light. This can be done with brushes and pens. Tooth brushes and old hog hair brushes are useful for achieving splattered and stippled effects (*Fig. 119*). Sponges and crumpled pieces of paper and material can be used for pressing on light-coloured textures. As a general rule, it is better to add more light detail and textures than you think you will need. Once the ink has been painted on, the light drawing and detail always seem to diminish in quantity and scale. If you do end up with too much light detail, unwanted areas can simply be painted out.

Once the masking fluid has been painted on, leave it to dry thoroughly. A fan heater can be used to hasten the drying time. When dry, hold the positive up to a light source to check the density of the image. Give any thin areas a second coat of ink. Again, leave to dry thoroughly.

When dry, the masking fluid is easily identifiable against the ink: it will look lighter in tone and be raised up above the surface of the ink. When totally dry, gently rub the masking fluid using the ends of your fingers. It will easily lift up and can be pulled away from the acetate in a series of strands.

When inking in the design,

119   *The light reversed-out areas of the positive were achieved by using masking fluid. Random half-tones and textures were achieved by splattering and stippling*

try to prevent the ink from forming puddles. These should be mopped up with a brush. Ink that dries in very thick layers will form a trap over the masking fluid, and difficulty will then be found in rubbing away and pulling up the strands of dry masking fluid. When all of the masking fluid has beeen removed, any of the remaining light areas can be reworked with ink. Finally, recheck the positive for density. Strengthen light areas with ink.

PRINTS FROM TONAL PENCIL DRAWINGS USING PHOTO STENCILS

An interesting and slightly unusual way of producing a print can be accomplished from the use of a single tonal pencil

drawing. For this you will require the services of a commercial photographer. From the drawing, he will be able to make a 12.5 × 10cm (5 × 4in) copy negative from which he can make a series of film positives, in register, on litho film. Each positive made, being exposed for a different length of time, will tend to separate out a varying proportion of the tonal image – the shortest exposure picking out only the darkest tones, and so on, with the longest exposure depicting the entire drawing, down to the lightest tones. The degree of tonality recorded on any one positive can be prejudged by initially making a test strip to record the effect of varying exposures.

The different positives made at the same time, from the one negative, are bound to be in perfect register with each other. Once this is done, a series of photo stencils can then be made and put onto screens in the

normal way. So long as the stencils are well made, they should provide the makings of a print, subtly different in character to that achieved through other methods of stencil-making. Some of the quality of the original pencil drawing should show through, achieving a concise, yet softened treatment of imagery. This, used in combination with an appropriate subject, for instance plant forms or an aspect of landscape, could greatly enhance the final result.

The kind of pencil drawing required to make a venture such as this worth while needs to be extremely clear and have a good degree of tonal finish and contrast. Working in this way, whilst being very time-saving and interesting, is nevertheless quite expensive on photographic services. A set of five or six in-register photo positives can be quite costly, and it is prudent initially to ensure that you make a pencil

121   July Meadow *by Nicholas Bristow*

120   Water Meadow *by Nicholas Bristow*

drawing that is worth working from. At the same time, you can produce a small image which will be much cheaper to process.

For the drawing, it is best to work on heavy good-quality cartridge paper with a matt surface. After mapping in the main shapes with a B grade pencil, you can start to develop the lighter tones. Try to keep in mind what the drawing is to be used for, work in a graphic way and keep the tones as even as possible. Always draw with well-sharpened pencils and keep a good degree of clarity throughout. 6B pencils are ideal for putting in the tones. Used on their side, with a little practice, you should soon be able to lay in flat areas of tone.

As far as possible, remember to build the drawing up in a series of different tones, instead of different tones running into each other and looking undecided. Crisp and straight edges of tone can best be achieved by working over an edge of taped-down tissue paper. Occasionally fix the drawing to prevent it from smudging, and use a sheet of clean white paper to shield the parts you are not working on at the time.

Certain subjects will obviously benefit more than others from this way of producing an image. Whilst this is mainly a matter of personal choice, complex imagery with a wide variety of tonality should work well. In the first place, a complex image will work just as well with this process as a simple one. But while simple designs can be produced using other means, by using complex designs you will be able to expand the imagery that you can use.

Secondly, images with a diversity of tone should print very effectively using this technique. The process will sort the tones out, giving you a series of photo positives that are in perfect alignment. The photo stencils will likewise print to a correctly-registered result, as long as proper printing procedures are kept to.

In printing from these various stencils, you will have to decide what tones and colours to use. To give substance to the overall design it might be necessary to make additional stencils. A master tracing can be made from some of the taped-down photo positives. From this, additional stencils can be simply made using any of the more standard processes. These can then be printed prior to the photo stencils to provide a basis on which to continue the print. Such additional stencils should provide added variation and depth of colour, without interfering too much with some of the more prominent printings made from the photo stencils.

OIL-BASED INKS

In recent years, technical advancement and improvements in both printing inks and screen meshes have largely transformed the screen printing industry. Whilst these benefits have been brought about with the bulk, commercial, side of the industry in mind, they nevertheless serve all printers and print-makers. Gone are the days when screen printing could necessarily be identified by thick clumsy coatings of printing ink. With the thin film oil-based inks now available, it is possible to print leaving ink deposits of one quarter thickness to those used previously, at the same time retaining equal covering power and intensity of colour. One advantage of this is the range of different effects obtainable in screen printing. It is now possible to use either thick or thin deposits of opaque or transparent colour. Printing can be carried out using fine detail and textural effects, or broad flat areas, according to need. Of printing methods, screen printing now possibly offers the widest choice of printed effects.

Apart from considerations of the medium as a whole, the use of oil-based inks allows a larger choice of techniques to be used. Tusche resist method, water-based cut film and photo stencil technique can be used with oil-based inks, but not with water-based ones.

Ranges of oil-based inks are available from most screen printing suppliers. They consist of finely-ground pigments in oil that can be thinned with either white spirit, or reducer. The initial cost of these products is less than that of tinters. However, in general they are far less versatile. The intensity of certain colours is weaker and they are often very opaque, which is a disadvantage where overprinted colour is concerned. They can be made more transparent when transparent base is added. Yet, at the same time, this has a weakening effect on the intensity of the colour.

Oil-based inks dry partly due to oxidation. They store well, providing they have airtight lids, and left-over colour can provide a useful basis for future prints. Large quantities can be stored separately. Small amounts, likely to dry out, are best mixed together to form new colours; in this way they will last for longer periods of time.

Different finishes and metallic colours

Oil-based inks dry to a matt finish. When numerous colours are overprinted, the resulting surface has more of a satin finish. Gloss finishes are best obtained by overprinting with one of the various varnishes available for this purpose. Ranges of extra opaque colours are also readily obtainable. They are useful for creating contrasting ink surfaces and for concealing printing errors, which, if necessary, can then be reprinted over. Metallic finishes are easily obtainable and work to good effect, due to the thickness of ink deposit. They can be made either with the use of metallic inks, or by using finely-ground metallic powder mixed into clear base. Transparent colours can then be overprinted to produce various effects of metallic colour.

Transparent base and reducer

Transparent base is an extender base that can be added to any oil-based inks and colours in order to reduce their opacity. Before being thinned, it is a sticky substance not unlike light-coloured treacle. Prior to use, it needs to be thinned with reducer and thoroughly stirred with a palette knife to an even consistency. When added to inks, it usually improves the consistency, making them flow more easily and making printing less difficult.

Used in combination with universal tinters and a tin of white, transparent base provides an excellent colour system for print-making. It is easy to use and takes up little room. With practice and patience, a diverse range of different colour effects can be obtained. Transparent base with a small amount of added tinters results in soft light colours and tones. Large amounts of added tinters can provide a range of vibrant transparent colours. Small amounts of white added to transparent base can be used to lighten tones and soften colours of preceding printings. Tinters,

122   *Transparent base and reducer*

with white added, can give a full range of opaque colours. Used with tinters, artist's oil colours are a useful source of extra colour. Earth colours, such as ochres or siennas, which are difficult to make from primary and secondary coloured tinters, can easily be supplemented in this way.

Universal tinters

Tinters are highly-concentrated oil-based colours, specially designed to strengthen and change other oil-based inks and transparent mixtures. They are usually available in a range of about ten colours, with at least one warm and one cool colour of each of the three primaries — red, yellow and blue. Although they are expensive, their powerful colouring capacity means that they last for a long time and are good value for money.

Procedure for mixing colours and transparent base

With a palette knife, scoop out some transparent base and place it in a clean mixing container. Add a little reducer and stir thoroughly. Continue to add reducer and to stir with a palette knife until the mixture is sufficiently thinned. A test of this can be made by holding the palette knife above the container: the transparent base should run freely off the end of the knife.

It is usually easier to mix the colours required on a glass slab, rather than add them directly to the base. In this way they are better mixed and more controlled. When mixing the colours, pour a small quantity of transparent base onto the slab and mix the colours into it. This can then be scooped up with a palette knife and thoroughly stirred into the transparent base. Do not judge the colour by its appearance in the mixing pot, but test it by repeatedly dabbing a small amount on test strips of paper. It is better to keep adding small amounts of colour and testing these, rather than add large amounts in the hope of getting the colours right the first time. Finally, when the colour is mixed, label it, writing down the colours used, in case you need to remix extra amounts later.

Sundries

Mixing and storage containers
You will need various mixing and storage containers, the size of which will vary according to the area of printing and the intended number of printings. It is important, for storage reasons, that the containers have airtight lids. Either empty metal tins or plastic containers can be purchased from screen printing suppliers. Screw-top jars can be saved and are useful for small amounts of colour. Cheap supplies of larger containers can usually be found locally. Many of the plastic containers I use were bought for a few pence from the delicatessen department of a large local supermarket.

Plate-glass mixing slab
A plate-glass mixing slab is a useful addition for mixing inks. Mixing and thinning colours on a slab, rather than adding pure colour directly to containers, ensures a more controlled mixture and prevents spots of pure colour remaining unmixed, eventually spoiling prints. Apart from buying new plate-glass, it is often possible to find pieces in junk shops, etc. Mine started life as a car window.

Palette knives
Large palette knives are needed both for mixing inks on a slab and for stirring up colour mixes in containers. They are also essential for collecting ink from the screen after printing. New palette knives can be obtained from any general print-making supplier. Old domestic palette knives, apart from being better value, are often more flexible, being made from tempered steel. They are especially useful for mixing colours on a glass slab.

Screen wash, rags and cleaning tissues
Screen wash is a powerful solvent used for removing either wet, or dry, oil-based inks. It can be purchased from

123 Falling Leaves *by Nicholas Bristow*

124   *Using a light box for trimming*

any screen printing supplier, usually in 5-litre (1 gallon) containers. Thick deposits of dried-in ink may require soaking for a time in screen wash to soften them before they can be removed.

Rags made from natural fibres are more practical for cleaning and removing ink: they absorb the ink more efficiently. An alternative is to buy industrial cleaning tissues from specialist manufacturers. Extremely absorbent, they clean more efficiently than rags, saving time and effort, which can help offset the cost. As a cautionary note, used oily rags should never be left around a printing area to cause a fire hazard. They should instead be kept in a metal container with a metal lid and be disposed of daily.

LIGHT BOX

Although a light box is not an essential piece of equipment, it is extremely useful as an aid to making stencils and photo positives. With the use of one, several cut stencils, or numerous acetate positives, can be aligned over each other to verify the registration and see how much overprinting will take place. A complete set of positives can also be taped down, positioned in correct registration, to have the edges retrimmed ready for printing (*Fig. 124*). When not in use, the top of a light box can be used

as a clean working top for design and other activities.

A light box should not prove too difficult to make (*Fig. 125*). For the frame, a sturdy table of working height with the top removed is all that is needed. Wooden batterns of 5 × 2.5cm (2 × 1in) can be screwed to the underneath of the top to support fluorescent light fittings. These are best placed at equal distance to achieve even lighting.

The top consists of two same-sized pieces of plate-glass, cut to the outside measurements of the table frame. In between the sheets of glass, place either sheets of tracing paper, or a piece of semi-opaque acetate drawing film. This is needed to diffuse the light, avoiding glare. Once the tracing paper is in place, the edges of the glass can be taped around with several layers of parcel tape, or carpet tape, to make them safe. If the light box is to double up in use for different activities, it may be worthwhile to cut a piece of

hardboard to cover the glass, to protect it when not in use.

LIGHT SOURCE

The photographic stencil process works through the use of ultraviolet light. A source of this is needed to harden the film emulsion. The cheapest source of ultraviolet light is direct sunlight, and whilst it could be used to make photo stencils, it is barely practical to do so. Apart from the length of time it would take to make the exposure, modern films require an exposure with the timing linked to a constant strength of light output, and sunlight is anything but constant. Photo flood lights are relatively cheap, but although they provide a constant output of ultraviolet light, it is quite weak, and exposure times are again lengthy. The longer the exposure time, the more the chances are that light will undercut the edges of the positive to leave the image ill-defined. While one can experiment with cheap light sources, it pays to buy a manufactured exposure unit. By doing this, you can at least expect high-quality well-defined stencils.

Exposure unit: mercury vapour lamps

The most practical and cost-effective light source is the mercury vapour lamp (*Fig. 126*). They are quite compact and can be bought from most screen printing suppliers as an entire wired assembly, with ballast, capacitor and fuses, etc. It is very important, for safety reasons, that they are wired correctly. The little extra you will pay for the finished unit should give you peace of mind as to the wiring. It can be safely plugged into a ring main.

A further cautionary note: when lit, do not look directly into the light source, as this will be damaging to your eyes.

When making the purchase, the supplier should be able to advise you on the strength of lamp needed for your requirements. The most widely-used sizes range from 125 watts to 400 watts. They give a good even light with a direct beam. The exposure time is relatively short. Before use the lamp needs to be switched on, with the shield in place over the light, for 5 minutes, in order to warm up. After use, it will not relight until the lamp has cooled. After 1000 hours of use, the lamp will lose power and longer exposures will be needed.

126   *Mercury vapour lamp*

Plate glass

Tracing paper

Plate glass

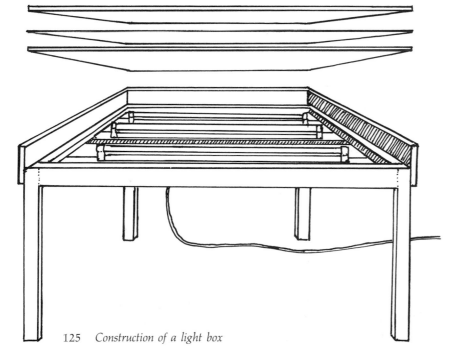

Fluorescent light fitting supported on battens

125   *Construction of a light box*

Wooden frame

Developer

The purpose of the developer is to harden the exposed areas of the film still more. It is always prudent to consult the film supplier as to the correct developer to use. Film can usually be developed in a solution of hydrogen peroxide. The strength of mixture, depending on the film used, is up to 2 per cent of hydrogen peroxide mixed in a water solution. However, developer, such as A + B developer, is usually more convenient to use. It is supplied in boxes containing small sachets of the two separate parts, marked A or B, of the developer. You simply have to tip the contents of sachets A then B into a pint of cold water, while stirring thoroughly. A milk bottle can easily be used for measuring out the water.

It is best to mix a fresh supply of developer each day. However, I have often used the previous day's mixture without any noticeable effects.

Exposure times and test strips

Exposure times will obviously vary according to the particular photo stencil film and exposure unit that you use. Maker's directions and instructions should provide an estimated exposure time, though this may have to be worked out by you from separate bits of information. However, the

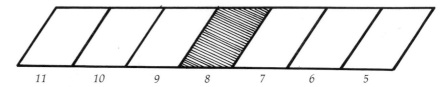

127a *Example test strip, with exposure times in minutes*

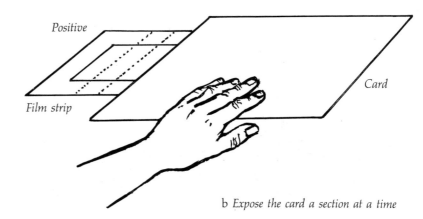

b *Expose the card a section at a time*

estimated time should not be taken for granted. It is important to find the correct exposure time, otherwise, loss of detail and poor definition can occur and the finished stencil may not adhere properly to the screen.

Finding the correct time is best done by making a test strip, similar to that used in photography. Use part of a positive and a strip of film to make a series of different exposures (*Fig. 127*). Make three exposures under the recommended time and three above it, with one minute intervals between exposures. Use, for example, an estimated time of 8 minutes. Firstly, place a piece of card over most of the film strip, exposing the small uncovered section for 1 minute.

Then move the card, uncovering a further section of film, and make another 1 minute exposure. Repeat this procedure until the seventh and final exposure, making this 5 minutes. You should now have a strip of film with seven different exposures, ranging from 5 minutes to 11 minutes. Develop and wash out the strip of film. From the results of this you should be able to judge the best exposure time. If still in doubt, process the film strip onto a screen and take a printing.

128 Late Summer *by Nicholas Bristow. Part way through printing*

129 Langhorne *by Jonathan Owen*

PRINTING DOWN FRAME FOR USE WITH PHOTO STENCIL FILM

When making an exposure for a photo stencil, it is vital that the acetate positive and the photographic film are held tightly together. The slightest gap between positive and film would allow light to under-cut the blocked-out image of the positive. This would result in a poorly-defined stencil, with distortions to the image and fine detail missed out altogether. The easiest and most economic way of providing a contact between positive and film is to use a sheet of foam and plate-glass (*Fig. 130*). The sandwich of glass, positive, photographic film and foam rubber sheet should ensure against movement and gaps. Weights placed around the edges of the glass, during the exposure, should further improve the contact between positive and film. However, to provide the best possible contact, a device called a printing down frame can be made or purchased.

Fig. 100b shows a home-made printing down frame. The vacuum pump can either be bought, or be converted from something else. Mine started life as part of a refrigeration unit, but a household vacuum cleaner might easily be used. The printing down frame consists of a flexible shallow tray, made of rubber, over

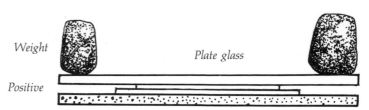

Weight Plate glass Positive Film

130a *Providing a contact between positive and film* Foam rubber sheet

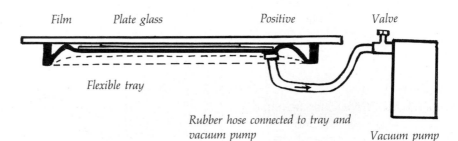

Film Plate glass Positive Valve

Flexible tray

Rubber hose connected to tray and vacuum pump Vacuum pump

b *Home-made printing down frame*

which rests a sheet of thick plate-glass. An airway connects from the base of the tray to a vacuum pump. The positive and film are placed in the tray underneath the glass sheet, ready for the exposure. When the pump is switched on, air is sucked from the tray, creating a vacuum. The flexible base of the tray is forced up against the glass, tightly sandwiching the positive and film against the glass. It is advisable to place a sheet of newsprint on the floor of the tray to prevent the film from sticking to the rubber during the exposure.

When the pump is initially turned on, you should press down on the plate glass to create a good air seal. When air has been expelled from the tray, you can release your grip. The

vacuum will hold the rubber edges tightly against the glass. Start the pump 5 minutes (the same time for which you turn on the exposure unit) before making the exposure. This will fully expel the air and make a good contact between positive and film.

On finishing the exposure, switch off the pump and release the air valve to allow air to flow back into the tray. At times, the rubber base immediately around the air outlet can prematurely press up to the glass, trapping air in the frame. To avoid this happening, place a small strand of wire on the inside of the base, overlapping the outlet.

WASHOUT UNIT

A shower attachment linked to

a hot water supply, to enable one to sprinkle hand-warm water over the film, is needed for washing out the stencil. One ready-made solution to this is to use a bath or the kitchen sink. However, this is not always desirable or convenient. If you have the room, a purpose-built washout unit is the answer. This can easily be constructed with three ply and wooden battening. When built, the inside joins between the plywood can be sealed with fibre glass tape and resin. Extra strength and waterproofing can be obtained by putting fibre glass matting and resin over the bottom of the tray and around the drainage outlet. The inside of the tray can then be painted with gloss paint. Painting the back of the unit white will make the stencil show up clearer during washing out, making it easier to judge the state of the stencil during the process.

A small electric water heater and shower attachment can be used for supplying warm water needed to wash out the stencils, while for cleaning screens, a garden hose with an adjustable nozzle and tap attachment is suitable, providing you have good water pressure.

Manufactured washout units are usually made from rust-proof metal and sometimes include illuminated back panels making screen inspection easier.

Photo stencil held in place with clips

Back painted white for easier screen inspection

Joins taped with fibre glass tape and resin, then painted with gloss paint

Bottom of tray and around water outlet covered with fibre glass matting and resin and gloss paint

Water outlet

Plywood

131   *Washout unit*

They are sometimes used in combination with high-pressure water units, which make screen cleaning easier by blasting a spray of cold water through the mesh (*Fig. 131*).

PRINTING PRESSES

The use of a printing press for screen printing is by no means essential. Yet, for a variety of reasons, the use of one makes printing overall an easier task. In principle, the workings of both manufactured press and home-made hinged screen and baseboard are much the same. They are both operated in a similar fashion; but here the comparison ends. Do-it-yourself woodwork cannot compete with precision engineering. Factory-built presses are highly-engineered structures which include a number of highly-useful refinements. They allow for greater accuracy of registration and faster printing.

For printing simple images in small editions, there would be little sense in justifying such a large expense. But, for printing complex images (using, for instance, finely-registered photo stencils) in large editions, the advantage is far more decided. An alternative to buying a factory-made press outright is to buy the parts that are impossible to make and then make up the rest oneself.

133   Late Summer *by Nicholas Bristow*

134   Sunlight on Farm Machinery *by Nicholas Bristow*

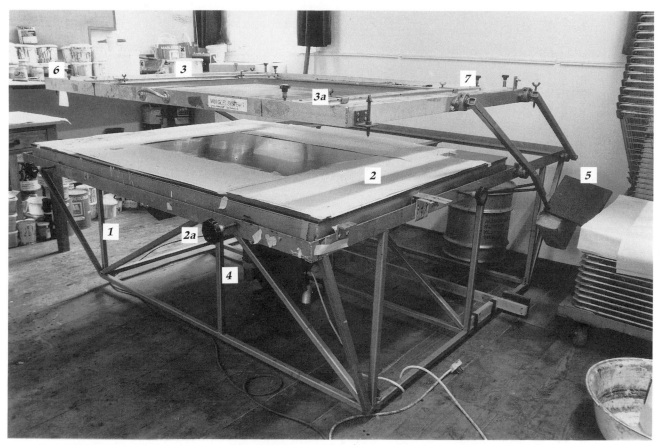

132 *Manufactured vacuum press*
1 *Frame*
2 *Adjustable vacuum bed*
2a *Fine alignment guides*
3 *Horizontal hinging mechanism*
3a *Mounting frame with screen clamps*
4 *Vacuum pump with automatic cut-out*
5 *Adjustable counterbalance weights*
6 *Alignment locating devices and frontal lift-off adjuster*
7 *Rear lift-off adjusters*

Manufactured vacuum press with horizontal lift hinging device

1 *Frame*

The frames of manufactured presses usually consist of strong tubular metal framework, with stove enamel finish, resistent to chemicals and water.

2 *Adjustable vacuum bed*

The purpose of a vacuum bed press is to hold the paper, or other printing stock, firmly in position and flat against the bed of the press during printing. The vacuum bed is best described as a large hollow flat thin box, with a series of small holes in the top and one much larger hole in the bottom. It works due to air being continually sucked out of the box, the suction holding the paper in position.

To start with, a sheet of paper, or card, is placed in position on the bed against three registration tabs. As the screen is lowered, the suction unit cuts in. Air is sucked through numerous small holes in the top of the bed, holding the paper in place flat against the printing surface. The stencil is then printed. As the screen is raised, the suction unit cuts out, releasing the print so that it can be removed to a drying rack. Factory-manufactured presses are usually designed with an automatic cut-out device.

The inside of the bed is honeycombed with small struts which support the top of the bed, while not impeding the flow of air within the box. The top of the bed is covered in a layer of strong plastic sheeting, providing a perfectly flat and easily-cleaned surface.

2a *Adjustable bed: fine alignment guides*

An adjustable printing bed allows for fine adjustments to be made to the registration, before and during printing. With better-made presses, there is usually an option to have a fixed, or an adjustable printing bed. For the average print-maker, working with numbers of overprintings, buying an adjustable bed is worth while.

An adjustable vacuum bed works by being balanced on special pads within a steel framework, and is held in place with metal springs. Three bolts, positioned one on either side of

135 *Two bars can be slid along the mounting frame and locked into position against the screen. Each bar has two screen clamps attached to it, with which to hold the screen firmly in place*

136 *Two horizontal bars run the width of the press, linking the jointed struts on either side*

the bed on the front framework, and one on the side, serve as fine alignment guides. To obtain correct registration, a taped-down master copy is first brought into alignment with the screen image by moving the screen within the mounting frame. When this is secured, finer adjustments are made by turning any of the three bolts. This gradually moves the bed, one way or the other, bringing the master copy into correct registration with the stencil. The use of retaining springs means that the bed will move back as the bolts are loosened.

3 *Hinging mechanism and mounting frame*
The hinging mechanism, which usually incorporates a mounting frame, is the most difficult part of a press to duplicate by do-it-yourself home-made means. Most factory presses are hinged at the back, by the means of two precision-engineered hinges linked by a metal bar.

The press illustrated in Fig. 135 is different in that it is hinged at the sides of the press by the means of two parallel struts at either side. Each strut is linked to both the mounting frame and outside frame of the press by two joints. Two horizontal bars run the width of the press, linking the two front struts and two rear struts on either side (*Fig. 136*).

The advantage of this system is that the screen can be raised and lowered in a horizontal position. This is extremely useful in that the ink will stay in the same position as the screen is raised or lowered, making printing and blended colours easier to control.

3a *Mounting frame*
The mounting frame is designed to accommodate any screen with dimensions smaller than the inner measurements of the mounting frame. Two parallel bars can be slid along the mounting frame to grip the edges of the screen (*Fig. 136*). Four screen clamps, attached to the bars, are then locked onto the frame to secure it. The bars are then locked into position, front and back, on the mounting frame.

4 *Vacuum pump with automatic cut-out*
The vacuum pump is connected to the bed of the press by a flexible extension hose that fits into a hole at the bottom of the bed (*Fig. 137*). Vacuum pumps,

137 *Vacuum pump*

139 *Alignment-locating device*

138 *Counterbalance weights*

140 *Foreground: one of four universal joints comprising the hinging mechanism Centre: vertical screw on left controls amount of rear lift-off*

like other parts of a press, can be bought separately. Factory-made vacuum presses are usually supplied with an automatic cut-out device. This works by either switching on and off the pump, or redirecting the suction away from the inlet on the bed of the press. For do-it-yourself enthusiasts, domestic vacuum cleaners are ideally suited for use as suction units for home-made presses.

5 *Counterbalance weights*
Weights placed on extension struts on either side of the hinging mechanism are used to counterbalance the weight of the mounting frame and screen (*Fig. 138*). They can be readjusted by being moved up or down the strut, to rematch the weight of different types and sizes of screens.

6 *Alignment-locating devices and frontal lift-off*
When the screen is lowered, it is important for registration purposes that it comes to rest each time in exactly the same position. To meet this requirement, alignment-locating devices are often fitted, towards the front, on both sides of the press. These devices can consist of two pointed bolts, fitted to the screen carriage, that locate as the screen is lowered into the corresponding holes set on either side of the press bed. As well as ensuring fixed alignment, these bolts can be adjusted up or down, and are used for frontal lift-off adjustment.

7 *Rear lift-off adjusters*
Two adjustable bolts, positioned on either side at the back of the screen mounting frame, act as rear lift-off adjusters (*Fig. 140*). This allows for the 'snap distance' (distance between the mesh and printing paper) to be altered.

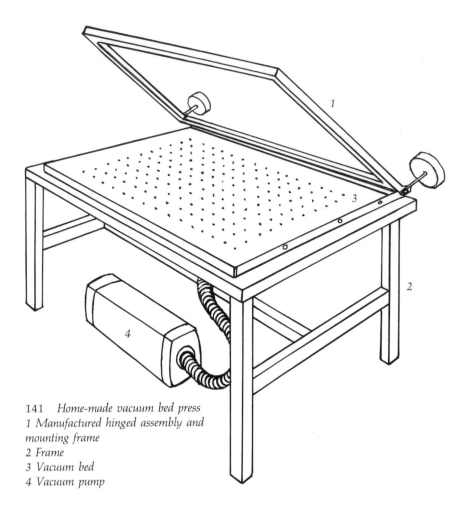

141 *Home-made vacuum bed press*
1 *Manufactured hinged assembly and mounting frame*
2 *Frame*
3 *Vacuum bed*
4 *Vacuum pump*

Home-made vacuum bed press with bought hinging mechanism

Apart from the hinging mechanism and mounting frame, it should not prove too difficult, or costly, to make a vacuum bed press. Both the frame and the bed require, at most, a rudimentary knowledge of woodwork. With time and ingenuity, it should be possible to adapt and make some of the refinements already mentioned of factory-made presses. The time and effort spent in making such a press would soon be repaid by the much-improved ease and quality of future printing.

1 *Hinge*
The hinging mechanism is the only part of a vacuum press that is difficult to make. Because it requires precision engineering, it is better to purchase a rear-hinged assembly with mounting frame.

2 *Frame*
The dimensions of the hinging assembly and mounting frame that you buy will determine the size of the press and the frame. The frame can easily be made from sturdy timber, such as 7.5 × 5cm (3 × 2in), or from bolted or welded angle iron. The top of the press should be made to a good working height. A top can be made from a piece of block board, with wooden struts underneath for extra support. Cut a hole in the centre of the top to take the vacuum cleaner hose.

3 *Vacuum bed*
The top and base of the vacuum bed can be made from

two equal-sized pieces of plywood. The top piece needs to have a plastic laminated surface. Nail and glue four pieces of 2.5 × 2.5cm (1 × 1in) battening around the edges of the base to form shallow sides of the box (*Fig. 142*). In the centre of a small piece of three ply, about 7.5 (3in) square, trace around the shape of the nozzle of the vacuum cleaner. Glue this to the inside centre of the plywood base.

Cut a hole through the base, the size of the marked-out shape, then nail and glue narrow battens, of 2.5cm (1in) depth, in a staggered row along the inside of the plywood base. They are needed for strength and support, but should not be placed in a way which would impede the flow of air in the box. Also, they must be placed so as not to overlap the grid of small holes in the top of the bed.

The grid of holes 2cm ($\frac{3}{4}$in) apart, should be marked out on the laminated top, and the holes drilled using a 2mm ($\frac{1}{16}$in) drill bit. Once this is done, the top of the bed can be securely glued and cramped to the base.

4 *Vacuum pump*
A domestic vacuum cleaner can be used to provide a very efficient suction unit. It will need to include a simple form of switching device; a foot-operated switch is preferable, as it leaves one's hands free.

An alternative method is to divert the suction away from the box. This can be devised by using a spring-loaded plate, with a hole in it. The plate is positioned under the press and suction outlet. By attaching a cable to the plate and part of the hinging mechanism, the solid part of the plate springs back over the vacuum outlet each time the screen is lifted.

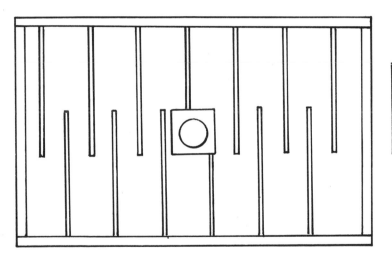

142   *Vacuum press. Base has battens in place, and a hole for the vacuum cleaner nozzle. Top has grid of small holes for air flow*

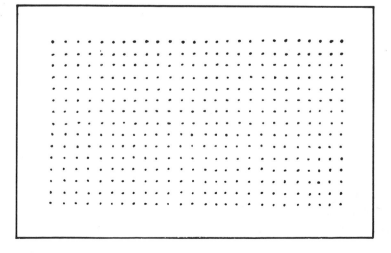

WORKSHOP LAYOUT

Workshop layout is an important factor in screen printing. Whatever available space you happen to have, whether large or small, it is a good idea to plan its use to the best advantage of the processes involved. By thoughtful and careful planning, a given space can be used to greater efficiency, thus resulting in a saving of time and energy, with possibly fewer mistakes made and less work spoilt. Likewise, general maintainance is an easier task in a well-planned print room. In achieving this, regardless of variables such as available space, cost, differing processes and personal requirements, there are several common conditions to keep in mind.

1   As far as possible, the layout should be designed to follow the pattern of the printing procedures. From the design and positives, through to making the stencils and the final printing, it is easier to work in a circuit, without doubling back too often.

2   The process overall can be seen to involve both clean and dirty activities. It is important that the areas where these two different types of activities take place should not be mixed up. Even if you have the smallest working space possible, the clean and dirty parts of the process need to be kept quite separate. For instance, it would not be advisable to attempt either mixing colours, or cleaning screens, in areas where paper is stored, or printing takes place.

3   Where necessary, safety precautions need to be taken

into account at the planning stage of setting up a print area, or studio. Materials and activities that could, if proper measures are not taken, present hazards should be properly dealt with. Chemicals, such as screen wash, should be stored safely, where there is no likelihood of them tipping over. Floor space, where you walk, should be kept clear of obstacles, such as extension leads trailing over the floor. Metal containers for oily rags, etc., need to be conveniently sited. Finally, activities involving harmful or volatile fumes should be carried out in areas close to adequate ventilation, such as a window, outside door, or extractor fan.

Whether working on a large or small scale, or printing large or small editions, the sequence of operations will be the same. By defining the various areas required for these activities to take place, some idea of how you can best plan your own layout should be gained. Since screen printing is the most adaptable of printing methods, it should not be too difficult to find a way around most problems. For instance, absence of space and facilities for a washout unit might easily be overcome by constructing a simple unit, with soakaway, outside to be used in conjunction with a garden hose.

In describing how a workshop could be planned and

set out to work efficiently, it is easier to have a particular example in mind. However, it would be impossible to conjure up such an example that, in itself, would be relevant to everyones needs. Instead, by describing how my studio space is divided and used, some idea of work sequences and planning should be gained.

The studio and printing activities

The arrows on the plan of the studio shown in Fig. 143 indicate the flow of activities, in chronological order, around the room. From design stage to finished stencil, the process follows a circuit around the studio, without doubling back on itself, to end up as finished stencils by the printing area. On the other side of the printing area, both printing stock and inks are close to hand. As the printing progresses, the prints circulate in a small area around the press, moving in turn from paper table to press, to drying racks and, when dry, back to the paper table, stacked ready for printing a further colour.

This kind of organization, or work flow, should avoid, as far as possible, confusion or mistakes occurring. The clean areas are set aside from those involving dirty activities. Where this is not possible, as with the paper table being close to the ink mixing area, extra

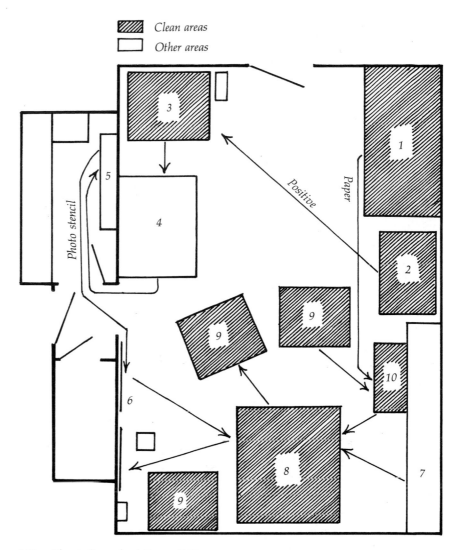

143   *The studio and printing activities*

1 Paper store
2 Design and positive making
3 Exposure unit and printing down frame
4 Developer
5 Washout unit
6 Screen drying and cleaning
7 Mixing inks
8 Printing
9 Drying
10 Paper and print table

precautions are taken. In this case when mixing inks, a large sheet of waxed paper is kept over the table, for protection. For the most part, the studio can be seen as being divided into nine main working areas, described below.

1   *Paper storage*
A built-in wooden unit, with open front shelving, used mainly for storing printing stock and newspaper. Large-sized finished edition prints are kept on shelving, enclosed in moisture-proof waxed paper wrapping. The thick plywood 2.5 × 1.2m (8 × 4ft) top is set at a good working height. This provides ample space for cutting printing stock to size, for proofing and editioning. The unit stands in a corner of the studio, fully separated from dirty areas such as colour mixing and screen cleaning.

2   *Light box*
Like the paper unit, the light box was purpose-built to fit into the working space. It is large enough to be able to hold A1-size positives, with enough surrounding space for inks, brushes and pens, etc. A tray is attached to one side for storing drawing and painting materials. The unit is used for making positives, lining up and trimming sets of positives prior to printing, and for general design work. Overhead spotlights, focused on the light box, are a useful addition when close registration and detail work are involved.

3   *Exposure unit and printing down frame*
Situated in another corner of the studio, the suspended exposure unit, vacuum pump and printing down frame are out of the way and take up a minimum of floor space.

4   *Flat working top for developing and processing stencils*
The 1.2 × 1.2m (4 × 4ft) working surface consists of a piece of white laminated chipboard which rests, at a good working height, on top of a large plan chest. The plan chest acts as storage for designs, positives, acetate film backing sheets, and an assortment of items from experimental prints to colour charts. The top is used for developing films, adhering films to screens, spotting out and applying screen filler to borders. Tusche resist stencils are also made in this area.

5   *Washout unit*
The washout unit is located

away from the main studio area, in a small room with a quarry tile floor, making clearing up an easy process. Apart from screen cleaning and washing out stencil images, the area provides a cool storage space for film containers. Having this facility set aside from the main studio means that the aggravation of having water puddled around is, to a large extent, isolated.

6 *Screen storage area*
This provides a safe area for screen storage. It is close enough to the press, yet far enough away from other activities to provide a clear space where screens are unlikely to become snagged or spoilt by other equipment. Screen wash is kept in this area, where it can be used for cleaning screens on the press and for removing dried printing ink from screens after used stencils have been removed in the washout unit.

7 *Colour mixing area and ink storage*
The colour mixing area consists of a long working top. A piece of plate-glass is used as a mixing slab for colour preparation. Stored behind this are ten tins of universal colour tinters. These, together with white, clear base and reducing medium, represent the main ingredients used in colour mixing. The ready-mixed colours are clearly labelled and stacked in plastic containers and large jars.

After editioning, left-over colours are stored under the working top, to be used in future colour mixes whenever possible. Every now and then stock is sorted through, and dried-up colour mixes are discarded. The underneath of the working top is also a storage area for empty colour containers, and new stock of clear base reducing medium and screen wash.

8 *Printing press*
The press was positioned to give adequate access on two sides, as well as generous working space at the front. Paper is fed onto the press from a table positioned to the side of the press.

9 *Drying racks*
Prints can quickly and easily be transferred to metal drying racks located in front of the press. Both racks have a fifty tray capacity. For large editions, or oversized prints, a third rack, at the side of the press, can be used. The racks are mounted on sturdy castors and can easily be moved around if necessary.

The main points to bear in mind, when planning the layout of a print area or studio, are practicality and efficiency, linked to available space and conditions. If space is limited, areas will have to double-up with multi-use. Cleaning can be done outside, and drying systems can be devised over-head with clips and lines.

MULTIPLE PRINTING FOR SMALL DESIGNS PRINTED IN LARGE EDITIONS

Printing large editions can be a very time-consuming and monotonous task. In this regard, the size of the print, or printed area, barely seems to matter. A small print will take almost as long as a large one to edition, for, although the handling and printing may be easier, the procedures of printing the various stencils are just the same.

One way of shortening the work load is to edition small prints in a multiple way. Instead of printing a single image at a time, print a number of identical images on one large sheet of paper. These can be placed in such a way as to allow for adequate borders around each image. The placing of the stencils can be worked out beforehand to allow for perfect registration, so that when each set of facsimile stencils over-print, they do so in alignment. As the printing progresses, instead of building up a single print, you can be, for instance, producing four facsimile copies, which, when finished, can be cut to size.

July Meadow, an A4-size print (*see* page 117), was printed in this way. Produced in an

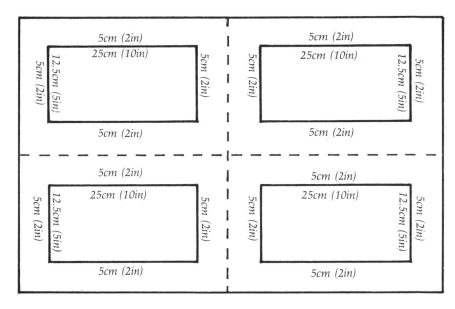

144   *Estimate of the overall printing size*

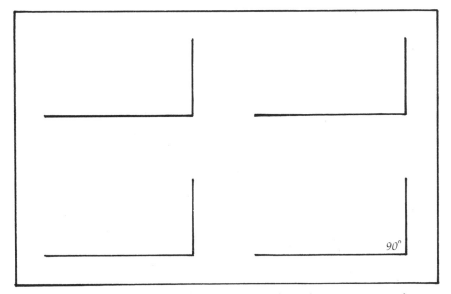

145   *Draw-in the bottom edge and right-hand side of each of the four designs.*

edition of 500, over 600 were printed to allow for wastage and misprints. The task of printing the design singly would not have been practical: printed using fourteen colours in nine separate printings, over 4,500 separate printings would have been required to complete the editioning. But, printed as multiples, four at a time, this was reduced to about 1125. I would not like to suggest that printing an image in multiples of four — four up — is anywhere nearly as easy as printing it separately, but it does not require much imagination to realize the saving in time, effort and patience that such a system provides.

The saving, by working in this way, can only be made by producing large editions. As the cost of having four sets of facsimile 'litho' positives made can be quite expensive, it is unlikely to balance against the time saved in the making of smaller editions. In such cases, it is possible to print a number of small different designs concurrently. By doing this, the same time saving can be gained when printing, and the extra costs are avoided. This will be explained later on in the chapter.

Procedure for aligning and printing four facsimile designs

1   Using a light box, register and cut to size your original set of photo positives. This is fully explained on p. 110.

2   From these, have four sets of SS (same size) lithos made up for you. An average-sized printing establishment, or commercial photographic studio, should be able to provide this service.

3   Tape down, in turn, each set of lithos to a light box, positioning them for correct registration. Using a steel straightedge and Stanley knife, recut the edges to just within the area of the design. Use a set square to ensure that the design is cut square. Keep the four sets of positives separate from each other. Also, keep each set in the order of printing, with the first four positives to be printed on top, and so on.

4   Work out the best positioning of the four images from a printing point of view. For printing straight colour, this will hardly matter, but, when blended colours are used, the designs will need to be

positioned in such a way as to print to best advantage. Once the positioning has been decided upon, the borders and paper size can be worked out.

5 Using a small piece of paper, estimate the overall size of printing paper required (*Fig. 144*). As an example I have used a print size of 25 × 12.5 cm (10 × 5in) and a border of 5cm (2in) all round. To guard against mistakes, it is easier to make a diagram similar to that illustrated.

6 Cut to size the required printing stock, estimating for wastage, such as damaged prints and misprints, etc.

7 Using one sheet of printing stock as a master copy, carefully draw in the bottom edge and right-hand side of each of the four designs (*Fig. 145*). This is best done with a clear thin pencil line. Use a set square to ensure that the lines are set square, at 90 degrees.

8 For each different colour stencil, or separate printing, you will need a sheet of acetate of the approximate size to cover the drawn-out lines on the master copy – in this case 66 × 41cm (26 × 16in). Acetate backing sheets left over from previous photo stencils can be used. Before use, wipe over both side of the backing sheets with a sponge and warm water to remove any traces of photo emulsion and dust, etc.

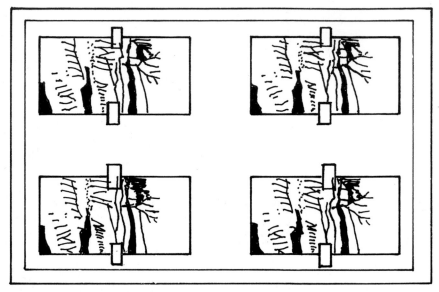

146 *Secure each set of positives with small pieces of clear adhesive tape*

9 Tape the master copy onto a light box. Then, tape the first sheet of acetate over the master copy. In turn, line up each of the first four positives to be printed over the acetate sheet. Ensure that the bottom and right-hand side of each positive exactly corresponds with the two drawn lines on the master copy. Using small pieces of clear adhesive tape, secure each positive to the acetate sheet (*Fig. 146*).

It is important that you do not mix up the sets of positives. Positives of any one set will only relate perfectly in alignment to that particular set. As you proceed, positives from a set should always be placed in the same order on the acetate sheets.

10 Remove the first sheet of

positioned positives, and secure the second sheet of acetate over the master copy. Position exactly and secure the second four positives to be printed. Continue with the same procedure until all the sets of positives have been correctly positioned against the master copy and secured to corresponding sheets of acetate.

11 A large photo stencil of each sheet of positives is then made in the normal way and processed onto the screen.

12 During printing, the sets of positives are taped, in turn, to the master copy. This is secured to the bed of the press. Then the screen stencil, bearing the four exact images, is aligned through the mesh to correspond exactly with the four positives.

147　Cabaret *by Nicholas Bristow*

148 *(Left)* Figure on a rug, *printed using a paper positive*

149 *(Above left)* Seated dancer *(paper positive)*

150 *(Above right)* Figures in movement *(paper positive)*

151 Standing Dancer *by Nicholas Bristow*

152   Seated Dancer *by Nicholas Bristow*

Explaining this process may sound complicated, but in practice it is very simple. It is mainly a question of care, in aligning the various sets of positives, and making sure that they are accurately set out. Perhaps the answer is not to be too ambitious to start with. Try an image designed with limited colour; this will be easier and, by using fewer sets of lithos, will also be cheaper.

Multiple printing incorporating different designs

Apart from printing multiples of the same design on a large sheet of paper, it is possible to print a number of totally-different designs at the same time, the only common factor being the use of colour. In general, the different images would need to be designed to use a common sequence of colour printings. This is not a particularly difficult problem. With the use of blended colour, it is even possible to print the two images on one side of the screen in one colour, while the other two are printed in a totally different colour. This method of working is highly suited to small items, such as greetings cards, as well as to limited editions.

A series of zodiac signs were designed and printed in this way. The first six designs were printed as a block on sheets of B1 (27.5 × 39in) paper,

153 Waggles asleep, *printed using a paper positive*

in five separate printings. Blended colour was used throughout to add variety of tone and colour. In parts, a softened effect was achieved with the use of fade-outs, made with extra clear base medium. The slightly mottled effect of colour was a result of using a textured Fabriano paper to print on.

For each design, positives were cut from red mask using a master tracing for guidance. On completion, each set of positives was taped down in alignment to a light box and cut to size, after which the same procedure as already described for facsimile designs was used to align the various positives onto sheets of acetate. Registration prior to printings was also done in a similar way.

In either case — of facsimile designs or different images — alignment of positives on the acetate sheets needs to be done concurrently. If too much time elapses between setting out the acetate sheets, atmospheric changes could affect the master copy; being made of paper, it could shrink or swell, altering the alignment of subsequently-registered positives.

Also, when printing multiple images, it is advisable to retain as constant a temperature as possible in the printing area. The registration of multiple printing is more critical, as sudden changes of room temperature are more likely to

show up in the finished results. For this reason, it is best to print during a continual time sequence. If you have to stop part way through editioning, it is prudent to store the unfinished prints wrapped in a large sheet of water-proof waxed paper. In this way the paper should not alter shape.

POSTERIZATION AND MEANS OF PHOTOGRAPHIC TONAL SEPARATION

Due to the nature of screen printed effects, resulting in flat, even colour and tone, it is difficult to achieve anything resembling tonal variation. Even with photographic means, it is impossible with a single stencil to do any better. Because of this disadvantage, a mechanical method called posterization has been developed for screen printing, which generally overcomes the problem. Instead of printing varied tones in a single printing, a range of different tones are overprinted, using a specially-adapted series of separate stencils.

First, a number of positives are made from the finished art-work using a range of different fixed exposures. Each exposure defines a differing amount of tone: long exposures define all of the tones, including the lightest; a mid-length exposure will leave out lighter tones, collecting half tones and darks,

and a short exposure will define only the darks. The positives are usually made using orthochromatc film. This is a high contrast film that converts the artwork into either black or white (clear plastic film backing). As to whether a particular tone will appear black or clear, this depends partly on the density of tone in the art-work and partly on the length of the exposure used. The line positives (solid tones as opposed to half toned positives) print to a good density of ink, fitting in well with hand-produced positives According to the image used, it should be possible to separate out up to four to eight different tonal stencils.

Second, the stencils, made from the positives using standard photo stencil technique, are printed using differing strengths of the same colour ink. The heaviest stencil, incorporating the lightest tones, is printed in the lightest ink, and so on, until the stencil with the least imagery is printed in the darkest toned ink. The printing is always made in a reversed progression of tones — heavy stencil, light-printed tones; light stencil, dark-printed tones. The resulting overprinting of the various stencils in different tones provides a very effective illusion of tonal variation. However, in achieving this, great care needs to be practised

154 Chinese Lanterns *by Nicholas Bristow*

155   *Paper collage of* Reclining Figure *by Nicholas Bristow, used as starting point*

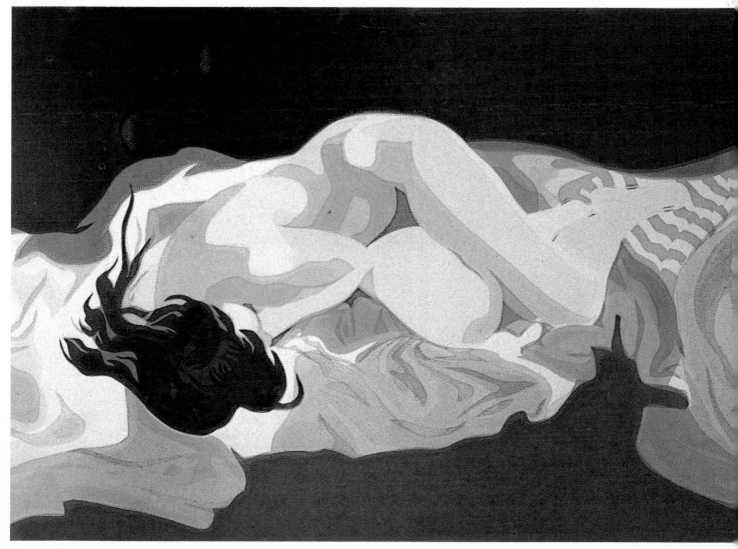

156   Reclining Figure *by Nicholas Bristow. Printed using six cut paper stencils*

in aligning the various stencils used. Accurate registration is essential.

By photographing the artwork using colour filters, the different colours – yellows, reds and blues – can be separated out onto a matching series of negatives. From these, sets of progressive tonal stencils can be made for each colour. By doing this, both the various colours and the different tones comprising any finished piece of artwork can be mechanically translated into a series of stencils, which can then be printed.

The technique also provides ample scope for individual interpretation and further development of imagery. The number of positives used for each colour and how each one is printed will play a role in the final outcome.

There is no need to keep to trichromatic colours. The posterized positives can be adapted and worked on by hand. Likewise, hand-drawn, painted and hand-cut positives can be made and used at any stage in the printing to modify, add to and enhance the image. With very complex images, a series of posterized stencils can act as a good basis for registration, saving much time in initially establishing the imagery, and making further alignment easier.

Making posterized positives is a highly-specialized field,

requiring professional skills and specialized equipment. Whilst it is possible to achieve some sort of result by amateurish means, it is hardly worth attempting this, other than for experimental reasons. It is better to take the finished art work round to a commercial photographer and have the positives made up for you.

FRAMING AND DISPLAYING PRINTS

With the arrival of such devices as the clip frame, there is some debate as to the best method of framing and displaying prints. Certain print collectors insist on

framing original prints with the entire border areas visible. The print is simply held in place between a sheet of glass, or perspex, and hardboard backing by a few clip devices. There are advantages to this system. Embossed marks, 'chop marks', placed by either artist, or publisher, on the bottom edges of the print border will be visible and the print will not look cluttered up by a mount and frame. For small prints especially, clip frames can provide a quick and cheap way of framing.

Sold in various standard sizes, usually relating to A1

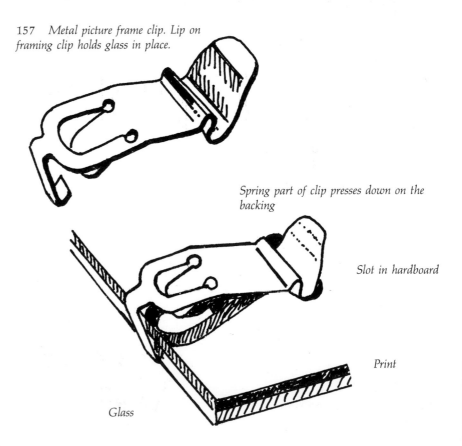

157 *Metal picture frame clip. Lip on framing clip holds glass in place.*

Spring part of clip presses down on the backing

Slot in hardboard

Print

Glass

paper sizes, clip frames comprise a piece of bevel-edged glass, a hardboard backing and several sprung clips (*Fig. 157*). They can be taken apart and reassembled, with a print in place, in a matter of minutes. The cord is usually hung from two clips. Odd-sized prints can be premounted on a frame-sized sheet of backing paper. An added advantage is that the frames are packaged in strong cardboard boxes. These come in useful when prints need to be carried around for exhibition purposes.

Also readily available are ranges of standard-sized metal-sided frames, the corners of which slot together and are held in place by small brackets and screws. They take a little longer to assemble than clip frames, but are still easy to use.

The more traditional method of framing, with a mitre-edged card mount and wooden moulded frame, is still a highly-favoured option. A bevel-edged mount not only offsets the print in a decorative way, it also permits air to circulate between the glass and print. Under certain conditions, prints framed directly against the glass have been known to deteriorate.

The main objective, when choosing a mount and frame, is to choose colours and styles that will offset the particular print, but at the same time not be distracting. When mounting

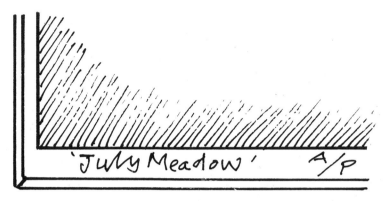

158 *Leave adequate space between the bottom of the print and the lip of the mount*

a print, it is usually best to retain a wide border. It is a fallacy that small prints require only a narrow border – often they need an even larger one. As a guide, keep the border width of the mount to at least 7.5–8.5cm (3–3½in), with an extra 6–12mm (¼–½in) added to the bottom margin. This will prevent the print looking as though it is falling down in the frame.

When cutting the mount, do not take the inside bevelled edge of the mount up to the print itself. Allow some space between the mount edge and the printed image (*Fig. 158*). The top and side edges will need at least 6mm (¼in) between mount and image; the bottom edge will need more. This is firstly to include the title, number (if it is a limited edition) and the signature.

159 *Cross-section of hockey stick shape of moulding*

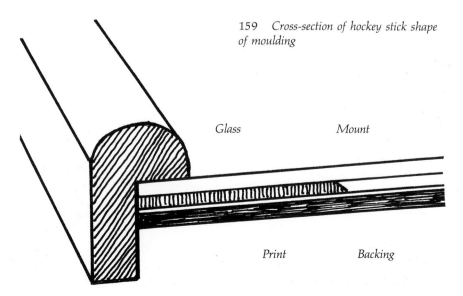

Glass   Mount

Print   Backing

160 Siesta *by Nicholas Bristow. Printed from six cut red mask photo-stencils using blended colour*

161   Geese *by Nicholas Bristow. The flat*
printed colours of the geese contrast
against overprinted foreground texture

Secondly, it will give the print
a better sense of balance. If you
are unsure as to the tone of the
mount, choose an off-white
ivory-toned mount, which will
suit almost anything.

The style and finish of the
picture moulding is very much
a question of personal taste.
What suits one person will not
necessarily suit the next.
However, in general terms, it is
always preferable to choose
simple uncluttered mouldings,
whatever the finish. Fussy and
complicated mouldings usually
manage to distract one's eye
away from the print. If
undecided, a plain hockey stick
cross-section moulding (*Fig.
159*), will make a good standard
frame, suiting most types of
print.

162   Shrubbery Road *by Clive Miller*

163　Morning *by Nicholas Bristow. Printed using nine photo-stencils*

164　Marshes in Winter *by Nicholas Bristow. Printed using five tusche resist stencils and four photo-stencils. The* photo-stencils *were made from a single photo-positive that was reworked for each stencil. By redrawing or scratching away* *parts of the positive, the image could be changed while still preserving perfect registration.*

TOWARDS THE FUTURE

Whilst new materials, methods and technology have greatly advanced the possibilities of the screen printing medium in recent years, research is still pointing in new directions. Work is at present being carried out by major manufacturers to develop a practical water-based system of inks. Easier to use, this would also dispense with the needs of many toxic and flammable materials presently needed, thinners and cleaning fluids in particular. Up to now, new materials and technology, developed for the commercial printing sector, have been just as useful to fine art screen printing needs. As to whether this will continue to be so with future developments, only time will tell. Whether or not any future ranges of water-based inks will have the necessary richness of colour and fullness of tone, suitable for fine art printing, we will have to wait and see.

Whatever the outcome, the materials and technology in present use are constantly being used and tried in different and new ways. The development of posterization in recent years is being used, in combination with hand-produced stencils, to create qualities and effects that would have been impossible only a few years ago. The adaptability of the medium continues to grow, borrowing from new ideas and art forms. Images derived from laser scanning technology and computer graphics are now commonplace. At the same time, and due to the flexibility of the medium, hand-produced methods can still be used in combination with modern advances to produce imagery and prints of extremely high quality and personal identity.

GLOSSARY

Alignment blocks   small pieces of wood, fixed to the sides of the baseboard, that keep the frame in line with the baseboard and in **registration** with the print.

Angle irons   flat pieces of L-shaped metal used to strengthen the corners of wooden printing frames.

Baseboard   a flat board that serves as a fixed printing bed to which screens can be attached.

Binders   mediums that provide body to dyes and inks and act as fixing agents.

Bleeding   the fault of ink seeping under the stencil during printing and spoiling parts of the image.

Block out medium   lacquers and other mediums used to block out parts of the screen to make direct stencils.

Chop mark   embossed mark placed on the bottom border of a print to identify the artist, printer or publisher.

Counterbalance   weights used on a press to offset the weight of the screen and mounting frame.

Counterchange   to alternate tonal values within a design, e.g. from light against dark to dark against light.

Cross hatch   regularly crossed over parallel lines to create various effects of tones and shades.

Deckle edge   the uneven edge characteristic of hand made and mould made papers.

Degreasing   removing traces of grease from the screen prior to securing a stencil.

Drying in   a state where ink has started to dry onto the screen, causing the mesh to clog and resulting in loss of detail and poor definition.

Editioning   producing a number of finished prints.

Flooding   pushing the squeegee back across the screen to ink it before printing.

Hot press   paper with a smooth surface finish.

Image   a design or drawing.

Lift off   the space between the screen and the printing bed that ensures the screen mesh progressively lifts away from the paper during printing.

Logo   letters or a symbol used to form a personal mark.

Masking fluid   a product that can be used on positives to achieve reversed out effects of drawing.

Master copy   a finished drawing, design or photo positive from which a set of stencils can be made.

Mesh   fabric that is stretched onto the frame to produce the finished screen.

Mesh bridging   the way in which a stencil crosses the open weave of the mesh.

Mesh count   the number of threads per centimetre or inch in a screen fabric.

Monochrome   one colour or tones of one colour; a design built up on the basis of tones of one colour.

Monofilament mesh   a screen fabric made from single strand threads.

Mutifilament mesh   a screen fabric made from threads consisting of several twisted strands.

Photo positive   a finished drawing or design usually made on acetate from which a photo stencil can be made.

Posterization   a photographic method of gaining the effect of varied tones by means of making a series of different timed exposures from a transparency; solid stencils made from these, when printed, can simulate multitoned effects.

Printing bed   the flat printing surface of a screen printing press.

Proofing   the stage of making a number of trial prints to judge the final result prior to editioning.

Snap   the action of the mesh continually lifting away from the paper during printing.

Squeegee   the flexible blade and holder used in screen printing to force the ink through the screen fabric.

Stock   the material such as paper, used for making the print.

Tinters   highly concentrated colours that can be used to adjust other inks or can be mixed with a transparent base to provide a wide range of colours.

Tooth   an action to roughen the surface of the screen prior to adhering a photo stencil.

Tusche   an oily lithographic ink used in screen printing as a resist method of making direct stencils.

SUPPLIERS

BRITAIN

General
Dane & Co Ltd
1–2 Sugar House Lane
London E15 2QN
(01) 534 2213

E.T. Marler Ltd
Deerpark Road
London SW19 3UE
(01) 540 8531

Pronk, Davies & Rusby Ltd
90–96 Brewery Road
London N7 9PD
(01) 607 4273

Selectasine Ltd
65 Chislehurst Road
Chislehurst
Kent
(01) 467 8544

Sericol
24 Parsons Green Lane
London SW6
(01) 736 8181

Serigraphics
Fairfield Avenue
Maesteg
Glamorgan
Wales
(0656) 3171

Paper
Atlantis Paper Co.
Gullivers Wharf
105 Wapping Lane
London E1 9RW
(01) 481 3784

R.K. Burt
37 Union Street
London SE1
(01) 407 6474

Falkiner Fine Papers
4 Mart Street
London WC2E 8DE
(01) 240 2339

Printing presses
Adelco Screen Processes Ltd
Weydon Lane
Farnham
Surrey
(02527) 23574

Samco Strong Ltd
PO Box 88
Clay Hill
Bristol BS99 7ER
(0272) 656271

Printing inks
John T. Keep
15 Theobalds Road
London WC1X 85N
(01) 242 7578

Fabric inks/pigments
Hays Chemicals Ltd
Bagnall House
55–57 Glenall Road
London SE15 6NQ
(01) 639 2020

AMERICA
Naz-Dar Co. of New York
45–46 39th Street
Long Island City
NY 11104

Atlas Screen Printing
Supplies Inc.
1733 Milwankec Avenue
Chicago
IL 60647

Cudnor & O'Connor Company
4035 West Kinzie Street
Chicago
IL 60624

Advance Process Supplies
400 N. Noble Street
Chicago
IL 60622

Colonial Printing Ink Corp.
East Rutherford
NJ 07073
800-225-0841

Cincinnati Printing & Drying
Systems Inc.
1111 Meta Drive
Cincinnati
Ohio 45237

Process Supply Company
986 Hanley Industrial Court
St Louis
Missouri

Stencil film, developer etc.
Ulano
210 East 86th Street
New York
NY 10028

INDEX